LIFE FROM OUR LAND

Marcus Grodi

LIFE FROM OUR LAND

IGNATIUS PRESS   SAN FRANCISCO

Cover photograph:
Ohio Farmland
© Shutterstock/Cynthia Kidwell

Cover design by Davin Carlson

© 2015 by Ignatius Press, San Francisco
All rights reserved
ISBN 978-1-62164-023-3
Library of Congress Control Number 2014959902
Printed in the United States of America ∞

It is when I possess least that I have the fewest worries, and the Lord knows that, as far as I can tell, I am more afflicted when there is excess of anything than when there is lack of it.

—Teresa of Ávila, *The Way of Perfection*

Property, wealth, diversions, amusements are often obstacles to the attainment of truth, beauty, celebration, delight, and love. They are not evil in themselves, of course, but the fact is that they allure us to fasten on them for themselves. They become finite crutches that distract and lead us away from our genuine quenching. Pulled to them, we cannot be pulled to God.

—Thomas Dubay, *Happy Are You Poor*

There are two wings that raise a man above earthly things—simplicity and purity. Simplicity must inspire his purpose, and purity his affection. Simplicity reaches out after God; purity discovers and enjoys Him.

—Thomas à Kempis, *The Imitation of Christ*

See that your praise comes from your whole being; in other words, see that you praise God not with your lips and voices alone, but with your minds, your lives and all your actions.... You cease to praise God only when you swerve from justice and from what is pleasing to God. If you never turn aside from the good life, your tongue may be silent but your actions will cry aloud, and God will perceive your intentions; for as our ears hear each other's voices, so do God's ears hear our thoughts.

—Augustine, *A Discourse on the Psalms*

I give to you forever this land of Narnia. I give you the woods, the fruits, the rivers. I give you the stars and I give you myself.

—Aslan in C. S. Lewis' *The Magician's Nephew*

CONTENTS

PREFACE

Then they were glad because they had quiet, and he
brought them to their desired haven.

—Psalm 107:30

"Our family left the city for the
country." So begin dozens if
not hundreds of books written
and published during the past
seventy-five years, all in the
aftermath of the experiences of
thousands of idealistic back-to-
the-earth folk seeking a simpler
life. This short book, however,

is not a journal or an autobiography about my family's move to
our rural land far off the beaten path. If it were, a better title might
have been *Life on Our Land*. Though this book does include auto-
biographical snippets, I do not intend to give here a running account
of our successes and failures; for that you can watch old episodes of
Green Acres or peruse the many books and websites on this topic.
Five of my favorite books include two classics entitled *The Egg
and I*, by Betty MacDonald (Lippincott, 1945), and *We Took to the
Woods*, by Louise Dickinson Rich (originally published 1942); and
three more recent publications, *Up Tunket Road*, by Philip Ackerman-
Leist (Chelsea Green Publishing, 2010), *The Dirty Life*, by Kristin
Kimball (Scribner, 2011), and *Growing a Farmer: How I Learned to Live
Off the Land*, by Kurt Timmermeister (W. W. Norton, 2012).

Nor is this book an apologetic for leaving the city for a self-
sustaining, off-the-grid, nonelectric, rural life of farming. Again,
there are many books, good and not so good, promoting this agenda,

by great rural-life apologists like Gene Logsdon, Joel Salatin, David Kline, Louis Bromfield, Wendell Berry, and Eric Brende. Four of my favorites of this genre are *The Contrary Farmer,* by Gene Logsdon (Chelsea Green, 1995); *Folks, This Ain't Normal,* by Joel Salatin (Center Street, 2011); *Small Is Beautiful,* by E.F. Schumacher (originally published 1973); and *Small Is Still Beautiful,* by Joseph Pearce (Intercollegiate Studies Institute, 2006). I suppose a little of this comes through in my writing, but this is far from my intent or agenda.

Neither is this a book about how to farm! Fortunately, there is an endless supply of books and websites on that topic, many of which I have consulted over and over and yet have only scratched the surface of what it means to be a farmer. My favorite books on farming are by authors such as Logsdon, Salatin, Karl Schwenke, Eliot Coleman, Brett L. Markham, Carla Emery, Richard W. Langer, Carleen Madigan, Tanya Denckla, Julius Ruechel, and Dirk van Loon. Two that I particularly enjoyed are the classic *Five Acres and Independence,* by M.G. Kains (Greenberg, 1935), and *Memories of a Former Kid: Once Upon a Time on the Family Farm,* by Bob Artley (Voyageur Press, 1978). There are far too many helpful websites to list here, so I'll mention just a few favorites: *The One-Cow Revolution, The Distributist Review, Callens Honey Farm,* and *New Catholic Land Movement.*

I've entitled this book *Life from Our Land* because I want to share what we have learned about life and, maybe more importantly, what we have discovered about how we ought to be living our lives, from having the privilege of living out here on our land. It may be that I could not have discovered most of this if I had remained in the city, but this is only because of the depth of my own obtuseness. You might already know all of what I hope to say and likely more, and have discovered it right where you are living now, in a twentieth-floor condo, at a busy intersection in downtown Cleveland. But just in case you don't, I'm passing these thoughts along for your consideration, comment, and critique.

For years I thought there was nothing new under the sun, but then I started paying attention to the landscape, the geography, and the rhythms around me. It not only awed me; it also helped me to see how God works through creation. I'm a believer! But I'm also a forgetter, and I have come to realize that nature is a great reminder. I am sharing this as a fellow traveler, hoping that we can help each other proceed more faithfully as we walk along together, through what I believe is a very difficult and precarious age, to our final destination.

Because I've always been a voracious reader, it's often difficult to pinpoint the sources of many of my reflections, but there are two books (besides the Bible) that have had the greatest impact on my thinking. The first is an ever living classic: Thomas à Kempis' *Imitation of Christ*. The second is a contemporary that I think should become a classic: Thomas Dubay's *Happy Are You Poor*.

The list of those I would like to thank, whether living or dead, is nearly infinite. Mostly I want to thank my wife, Marilyn, who, in addition to standing beside me (and doing her best to put up with me) through all of this, made this book far more accurate and readable through her proofing; my sons, Jon Marc, Peter, and Richard; and the precious new additions to our family, Teresa, Dominic, and Lucy, who also have shared this continuing journey with us. I also am grateful to Marilyn's sister, Holly, and her helper and friend, Tiny, for their insight into and assistance with all aspects of our acclimation to life on this land. We thank the cattle, sheep, pigs, chickens, cats, dogs, horse, and myriad of birds that have provided the challenges of this rural experiment, but I presume it will be many years before this text will be translated into their dialects. Also, I am eternally grateful for the editorial corrections and comments of Jeanette Flood. To the extent that this former sow's ear collection of articles has any semblance to a silk purse is due mostly to her editorial skills! I also especially thank my staff at the Coming Home Network International who have bandied my ideas about, helping me hone them into something more presentable. And finally, my thanks to our many good friends who, like my family and me, are trying at different levels to fight the good fight of the faith in our modern culture, both in rural and city settings: the families Cross, Madrid, Ryland, Cano, Horn, Moses, Dougherty, Evans, Hahn, Welker, Pearce, Sullivan, Ellis, et cetera, et cetera.

As I invite you to consider a few things we've learned about "life from our land", allow me to quote Louise Dickinson Rich from her classic description of their retreat to the woods. You might consider this the caption to our photo at the beginning of this Preface: "Why did we come to live here in the first place? We thought it was because we liked the woods, because we wanted to find a simple, leisurely way of life. Now, looking back, I think that we were unconsciously seeking to find a lost sense of our own identity.... I know that many people—perhaps most people—couldn't feel that, living here, they held within their grasp all the best of life. So for them it wouldn't be the best. For us, it is."[1]

[1]Louise Dickinson Rich, *We Took to the Woods* (Rockport, Maine: Down East Books, 1970), pp. 319, 322.

Weed 'Em & Reap

Weed 'Em & Reap is the unofficial name of our twenty-five acres. The problem is, so far we've mostly reaped only weeds.

It was never our articulated dream to move to the country, let alone attempt anything close to farming. Twenty-eight years ago, when Marilyn and I became one in marriage, we lived in the parsonage owned by the small Presbyterian church that I was pastoring. After that followed our first three personally "owned" homes, all in suburbs or neighborhoods, and we enjoyed the camaraderie of good neighbors. Then, to our sorrow, Marilyn's beloved grandfather died. This led to the dividing up of the century-old family farm. To Marilyn's surprise, we received ten acres of entirely rolling, mostly wooded, and predominantly clay Appalachian foothills. We weren't immediately certain what God was trying to tell us, but in time, we put our heads together, designed a saltbox-style cedar home, had a local contractor build what we had designed (with many modifications), sold our house in the city, and with our three sons moved out to the woods.

I say woods, because even as we distributed ourselves and our belongings into our fresh new country home, I had nary an inkling about farming. Although Marilyn's grandparents were farmers, I have had no farmers in my bloodline for at least three generations, and my only connections with the farm as a snotty city kid involved eating its produce and ridiculing Future Farmers of America (FFA) students (Father, forgive me, for I knew not what I was doing).

I came barely equipped with gardening experience. As a young only child, living with my parents on a half-acre city plot, I once became inspired to plant a garden. I mapped out a thirty-by-fifty-foot section and, on a hot, humid day in June, began my first trek with a rototiller. I made a fifty-foot swath down one side of the envisioned garden, which happened to be directly down the center of the yard. At the other end, exhausted and sweaty, I struggled to turn the machine around. As I started the second row, the voice of my next-door neighbor pierced through the loud din of the motor, reminding me that baseball practice started in ten minutes! I turned off the rototiller, grabbed my gear, and went to practice. I didn't return to the garden, though. The tiller sat there at the farthest end of our yard, through at least one rainstorm, until, under my father's "encouragement", I dragged it back into the garage. Baseball, swimming, band practice, and other more pressing interests drowned out my desire to finish the garden. Eventually that lone swath down the middle of our yard filled in naturally with grass and weeds, and to this day, anyone cutting that grass can notice a slight, inexplicable, fifty-foot-long dent.

I merely presumed that our move to the woods would be one long retreat—relaxing on our spacious porch, sipping sodas, keeping the bird feeders full, reading book after book, strumming my guitar on the porch without the worry of annoying the neighbors, maybe a daily jog or walk down our gravel road—but there it was, about three hundred yards away, across the valley: a hundred-year-old sheep barn, built by the skilled hands of Marilyn's great-grandfather and grandfather. Marilyn had insisted that we position our new house so we could look directly across the valley at the barn, but I'm sure

neither of us anticipated what
its presence there would mean.

One morning, not long after
moving in, when I was sitting
on our porch looking out over
the valley, it occurred to me that
that barn had been made for a
purpose. In the same way that
a house without a family is not a
home, that barn, constructed by hand from wood harvested and
milled off this land, without critters or stacks of hay bales, was not
fulfilling its purpose. And this land, which had been hand cleared
by the first settler and his family less than two hundred years ago—
long before bulldozers, tractors, or chain saws—was not fulfilling its
purpose. Since these revelations, our lives have never been the same.

We haven't yet erected an arched stone sign telling our neighbors
the name of our land and likely never will, because to do so would
imply that we're serious about being farmers. I learned long ago that
I am far from worthy to be called a farmer. When I was a boy, I was
told that the definition of *farmer* is "a man outstanding in his field."
Well, now fifty-plus years later, I've certainly learned that there's a
lot more to farming than donning bib overalls and standing out in
a field!

What is our main crop, you ask? Well, during our first years here,
our only intentional crop was Marilyn's strawberry patch, which did
surprisingly well. Our bumper crops, however, have usually been
wild raspberries and blackberries, but our largest showings are still
generally ironweed, spiceberries, stinging nettles, and multiflora rose.

Some of you might be impressed, but any farmer would know
with a smirk that Weed 'Em & Reap "farm" is being run by a dis-
organized, ignorant, displaced city dweller. I could easily fill a book
with the mistakes I've made (not knowing until the surprise was in
my lap that our goat was pregnant; burying my tractor seat deep
in muck; "helping" our Jersey cow deliver her first calf only to find
myself deluged in afterbirth; and being thrown ankles over arm-
pits by an escaped pig), but there also have been many victories. By
God's grace and humor, my family and I have learned a lot, but more
importantly, we've enjoyed our life here on our land together.

What I have also discovered, and this is why I'm writing this book, is the real reason I have come to believe that God called us "out into the wilderness". I first thought it was as a retreat from the growing craziness of urban life, but that was not it. Then I began to wonder, given the gift of this land and that barn, whether it was to farm, particularly within the growing mind-set of sustainable homesteading. And I can't say we haven't tried. Over the years, we have invested a heap of time, talent, and money in improving this acreage into at least what more serious farmers would call a minimally productive "hobby" farm. This, however, was not the reason, either.

What I have come to believe was the real reason for our move to the country is what I'd like to share in this book—with the hope that maybe it will help you discover that the important truths of detachment and simplicity are not only for those who choose to leave the city for the country, to leave industry for the farm, but are precisely to be lived right now where God has placed you.

Many today are quite concerned, if not fearful, about the direction in which our nation and culture are headed. I have heard far more than a few express their desire to escape the trials and tribulations of the city, where they feel they have been "exiled", for the peace and safety of the country—as they presume we have. What is far more important, though, is to discern prayerfully where God has called each of us to live, and why. From where you sit, things might look and sound far more promising out where we live, but this is true only if God is calling you to move.

The prophet Jeremiah once wrote a letter to the Israelites who had been taken into exile from Jerusalem to Babylon. Certainly, their hope was to return to the Promised Land, but in the meantime, God gave them this message:

> Thus says the Lord of hosts, the God of Israel, to all the exiles whom I have sent into exile from Jerusalem to Babylon: Build houses and live in them; plant gardens and eat their produce. Take wives and have sons and daughters; take wives for your sons, and give your daughters in marriage, that they may bear sons and daughters; multiply there, and do not decrease. *But seek the welfare of the city where I have sent you into exile, and pray to the Lord on its behalf, for in its welfare you will find your welfare.* (Jer 29:4–7, emphasis mine)

If we truly desire peace and fulfillment in this life, it seems to me that the Lord is saying that we must first "seek the welfare" of the place where He has sent us "into exile", to "pray to the LORD on its behalf, for in its welfare [we] will find [our] welfare" (Jer 29:7). Only by gratefully appreciating and seeking His presence right where He has us now will we experience the blessings where He might call us tomorrow, for I can promise you that the beauty of this bed of roses in which He has called my family to live, out here on Weed 'Em & Reap "farm", has its fair share of thorns. And the biggest thorn for my family to bear is me. Lord, help us.

2

Look at the Birds

For all men who were ignorant of God
were foolish by nature;
and they were unable from the good things that
are seen to know him who exists.

—Wisdom 13:1

After that old barn, the next most striking aspect of our new rural life in this
encroaching forest is the birds. Since
our new house was built high on the
side of a hill, with a large second-story
deck, we look out into the treetops. We
essentially live in an aviary!

On nearly any day of the year, we
can relax to the sounds and sights of all
the birds of Midwestern America: rob-
ins, jays, and crows; red-tailed hawks
and circling turkey vultures; chickadees,
tufted titmice, and nuthatches; catbirds
and mockingbirds; rufous-sided towhees, scarlet tanagers, and Balti-
more orioles; hummingbirds, woodpeckers, and barn owls; and my
favorite, wood thrushes. Whenever I hear, on a spring evening, the
three mournful stanzas of the wood thrush's call, I feel as if a friend
has graciously chosen to return to his home on our property—or is it
our home on his property?

My sons and I have often, with binoculars in hand, braved our way
through briars in the quest of seeing with our own eyes the elusive

creature whose beautiful familiar call has beckoned us. Sure, we can look it up in a bird book or watch a PBS documentary, but I've tried to teach my sons the beauty of "catching" wildlife with our senses: seeing and hearing and, if possible, even touching these beautiful gifts of God's love.

Years ago I dabbled for a time in scientific materialism. I have always loved science, which led to my studies in college and years in industry. For several years, I abandoned my childhood faith and accepted the possibility that all life could be explained through biology, physics, chemistry, and mathematics; that the seemingly infinite diversity of nature could be simply explained through mutations, natural selection, and survival of the fittest, all given the miraculous ingredient of enough time.

Yet one of the things that helped me see the inadequacies of this mind-set was the miracle of birds, particularly the fact that each species has a unique song. Consider, for example, that every single prothonotary warbler in the world has not only the exact same shape and coloring but also the same unique song. For hundreds of years, ornithologists have distinguished bird species not just by their physical characteristics but by each specie's unique call—the phrase of sounds that each bird repeats. Some attribute this to Darwinian evolution, genetics, natural selection, and survival of the fittest, but I can't see how any of that clearly explains why and how every individual bird of a species around the world has the same song. All beagles may have similar sounding barks, but they don't all retort the same exact series of barks (e.g., two short low barks, then one long high bark, followed by a growl) every time they open their mouths. Through pious and humble reflection, this astounding fact can lead a person to appreciate gratefully the creative love of God, who, from the beginning of time, established His symphony of song in nature. Do you hear it? Do you stand in awe? Or do you ignore the miracle and merely jump into your car and, behind closed windows, speed off to work or your kid's soccer field?

Through His teachings, Jesus encouraged His followers to look around at creation for evidence of God's existence, love, and care. In His Sermon on the Mount, He said, "Look at the birds of the air: they neither sow nor reap nor gather into barns, and yet your heavenly Father feeds them. Are you not of more value than they?"

(Mt 6:26). In another place, Jesus made a similar comparison: "Are not five sparrows sold for two pennies? And not one of them is forgotten before God. Why, even the hairs of your head are all numbered. Fear not; you are of more value than many sparrows" (Lk 12:6–7). Jesus assumed that His audience recognized the beauty, order, and care of God in the lives of mere birds—but had they extrapolated from this the care of God in their own lives?

Great spiritual writers throughout the ages have likewise used nature as the starting point to prove God's existence and His intimacy. For example, Saint Bonaventure, in his *Journey of the Mind to God*, gave six steps toward achieving intimacy with God. The first step involves looking at the vestiges (or visible evidence) of God in His creation and recognizing the beauty, order, variety, et cetera as signs of His creative love. This was not a new insight by the great Franciscan philosopher but merely a reflection on what had always been clearly proclaimed in Scripture.

For example, King David opened one of his most famous psalms with the following affirmation, not of something new but of that which he assumed his audience already believed:

> The heavens are telling the glory of God;
>   and the firmament proclaims his handiwork.
> Day to day pours forth speech,
>   and night to night declares knowledge.
> There is no speech, nor are there words;
>   their voice is not heard;
> yet their voice goes out through all the earth,
>   and their words to the end of the world. (19:1–4)

Centuries later, the apostle Paul, building on this common assumption, wrote to the Roman Christians: "Ever since the creation of the world [God's] invisible nature, namely, his eternal power and deity, has been clearly perceived in the things that have been made" (Rom 1:20). God's people have always recognized that the evidence of God's love and His creative actions are clearly evident in the creation around us—if we are willing to look and *see*.

I have come to believe that a correct understanding, appreciation, and utilization of the world that we have been given to live in require that we recognize behind it the creative love of God. Without this, well-meaning people misunderstand this world and its resources and fail to appreciate and use them correctly.

The problem with far too many of the modern, well-meaning, back-to-the-earth, simple-life, sustainable-farming types is that they want to regain the simpler lifestyle of their grandparents on the farm without the foundation of their grandparents' faith—without their grandparents' ability to see the loving fingerprints of God in every-thing they possessed. Nearly all of our farming ancestors here in America were Christians, Jews, or Native Americans. They farmed with the underlying assumption that all they had was a gift of their Creator God; they were thankful when farming went well because they knew this was a gift of God's providence; and when things didn't go well, they still knew that all happened within God's mysterious yet merciful plan. Moderns, however, want the simplicity without their grandparents' undergirding faith and philosophy, and as a result, their goals and decisions are all too often misguided and misdirected.

Many centuries ago, long before modern, agnostic scientific mate-rialists promulgated the godless origin and meaning of our world, the writer of the book of Wisdom recognized the foolishness of this. What he said sounds amazingly contemporary:

> For all men who were ignorant of God were foolish by nature; and they were unable from the good things that are seen to know him who exists, nor did they recognize the craftsman while paying heed to his works; but they supposed that either fire or wind or swift air, or the circle of the stars, or turbulent water, or the luminaries of heaven were the gods that rule the world.
>
> If through delight in the beauty of these things men assumed them to be gods, let them know how much better than these is their Lord, for the author of beauty created them. And if men were amazed at their power and working, let them perceive from them how much more powerful is he who formed them. For from the greatness and beauty of created things comes a corresponding per-ception of their Creator.
>
> Yet these men are little to be blamed, or perhaps they go astray while seeking God and desiring to find him. For as they live among his works they keep searching, and they trust in what they see, because the things that are seen are beautiful. Yet again, not even they are to

be excused; for if they had the power to know so much that they could investigate the world, how did they fail to find sooner the Lord of these things? (Wis 13:1–9)

This confirms one of the reasons Marilyn and I believe that God called us to move our family from the city out to the woods—not to farm, mind you!—but to help our boys grow closer to God through the beauty and simplicity of His creation.

All Good Gifts

As I begin this book, it is appropriate to give credit to one of the first sources that opened my eyes to the connection between the world around us and the loving God who created it and gave it to us for our enjoyment. When I was young, my mother taught me a hymn that we often sang in our Lutheran church. It was based on a verse from the letter of James: "Every good endowment and every good gift is from above, coming down from the Father of lights with whom there is no variation or shadow due to change" (1:17).

Later I learned and sang a version of it from the rock opera *Godspell*, which I often have played on the piano and sung with family and friends. I get teary eyed every single time because the hymn means so much to me. It's not just nostalgia but the way the author so beautifully and creatively expresses how we should thankfully address our loving Creator Father for every single thing we have. It is all a gift, and I pray that the words of this hymn will help you appreciate your world and thank your Creator for it.

> We plough the fields, and scatter the good seed on the land,
> But it is fed and watered by God's almighty hand;
> He sends the snow in winter, the warmth to swell the grain,
> The breezes and the sunshine, and soft refreshing rain.

All good gifts around us
Are sent from heaven above;
Then thank the Lord, O thank the Lord
For all His love.
He only is the Maker of all things near and far;
He paints the wayside flower, He lights the evening star;
The winds and waves obey Him, by Him the birds are fed;
Much more to us, His children, He gives our daily bread.
All good gifts around us
Are sent from heaven above;
Then thank the Lord, O thank the Lord
For all His love.
We thank Thee, then, O Father, for all things bright and
good,
The seedtime and the harvest, our life, our health, our food:
No gifts have we to offer for all Thy love imparts,
But that which Thou desirest, our humble, thankful hearts.
All good gifts around us
Are sent from heaven above;
Then thank the Lord, O thank the Lord
For all His love.[1]

---

[1] Matthies Claudius, "Wir pflügen und wir streuen" (1782), trans. Jane M. Campbell; tune: *Wir Pflügen*.

3

Stewardship

By faith we understand that the world was created by the word of God, so that what is seen was made out of things which do not appear.

—Hebrews 11:3

As far as Marilyn and I can tell, until the early 1800s, no man, except perhaps a passing Native American hunter, had set foot on our piece of rural America. Until then it had been nothing more than a dense forest of enormous virgin trees (see Conrad  Richter's fine novel *The Trees*). Then, around 1825, a young pioneer and his family bought the land for five dollars from the new state of Ohio. Without any modern machinery, the pioneer built a log cabin, cleared the land to farm, and raised sheep to support his family. For most of the past two hundred years, this family's descendants and then the Shaws, Marilyn's maternal family, have been faithful stewards of this land, keeping it cleared and useful for farming. When we moved onto ten acres of this original homestead, and then expanded to twenty-five, we accepted this responsibility of stewardship.

The Good Book doesn't progress very far before it speaks of this responsibility for stewardship of this earth and all the creatures on it:

Then God said, "Let us make man in our image, after our likeness; and *let them have dominion* over the fish of the sea, and over the birds of the air, and over the cattle, and over all the earth, and over every creeping thing that creeps upon the earth." So God created man in his own image, in the image of God he created him; male and female he created them. And God blessed them, and God said to them, "Be fruitful and multiply, and fill the earth and *subdue it*; and have dominion over the fish of the sea and over the birds of the air and over every living thing that moves upon the earth." (Gen 1:26–28, emphasis mine)

There are many things that being created in God's image means; one in particular is that we are to be like Him and act like Him. Mankind has been created to have "dominion" over this world, and because we have been created in God's image this means a dominion of love, humility, and selfless giving. Likewise, this is how we are to carry out our responsibility to "subdue" the earth. The way God loves, cares, and provides for all of creation is to be our model—and how we imitate that model is, I believe, how one day we will be judged.

Stewardship is the responsibility to take care of what we have been given, because one day we will give it back to God. If you are not willing or don't feel able to take care of a hundred-, fifty-, twenty-five-, or even one-acre plot of rural land—and this includes all the "fish ... birds ... cattle ... and ... every creeping thing that creeps upon" that land—then this is probably a good sign that God has not called you to leave the cozy condo in the city for a piece of rural America.

Discerning Purpose

Not long after moving in and being awakened by the whisper of that hundred-year-old barn, I was walking across the back acres, wondering what would be the best use for this partic-ular piece of land. For over a hundred years it had been used

for grazing livestock, mostly sheep, but for the past thirty or so it had sat fallow. Occasionally the fields had been harvested into square bales of hay, but as I examined the mixture of grasses, briars, thistles, and weeds struggling for political influence, gerrymandering different sections into nonproductiveness, I wondered whether it would be best just to start from scratch.

The most distinguishing feature of this land is that it isn't flat, like the farmland around my childhood home in northwest Ohio; rather, it consists of rolling hills, woods, and creek beds. In considering what to do with this land, I began by consulting with the few neighbors who were still farming, but mostly I read shelves and shelves of books. At first, I found their suggestions instructive, even inspiring, but, in time, I felt paralyzed by a cacophony of opinions. Many of the authors' ideas seemed contradictory—old school versus new school—often applying universal solutions regardless of the lay of the land. Too often the well-meaning writers assumed that the recipient of their advice had no outside job and therefore plenty of time to dedicate to full-time farm work. The mistake was obviously more mine than theirs—I was too ignorant even to ask the right questions, let alone see the unity in their experienced advice.

As I walked those back acres, with a field to my right that desperately needed mowing and overgrown woods to my left that needed denuding of grapevines, it struck me how important it was first to distinguish the purpose of this land before considering what it could or should be used for. There is a danger in seeing this or any piece of land only from a utilitarian perspective before first recognizing its deeper, more universal value. Why is this land here? Why is this earth here?

If a person rejects the idea of a Creator and insists rather on a purely accidental, impersonal "big bang" as the origin of all things, then there are no grounds to presume any altruistic purpose or value to anything in this world. What difference does it make what anyone does with the land? Why preserve it or protect the wildlife that also consider the land their home? Why not squeeze from it every ounce of substance, gleaning the maximum profit, even if the land ends up nutritionally bone-dry?

Naturalists argue that we must preserve the land, its resources, and its wildlife for the good of mankind and future generations—but, from an atheistic perspective, why? I believe the naturalists' well-meaning goals are the voice not of reason but of conscience. Created in the image of God, every person has within his heart the memory of our primordial responsibility to be good stewards—to have dominion and subdue, to appreciate and care for this good earth in imitation of its Creator. We particularly see evidence of this primordial conscience, for example, in the primitive religion and values of our Native American predecessors.

Many naturalists, however, argue that it was Christians, with their supposed God-given right to dominate and subdue, who have denuded the land, creating irreversible imbalances in nature, all for the sake of profit and self-gain. And sadly, they are right, for far too many Christians have done this, and continue to do this, out of a twisted utilitarian work ethic. We have too often misinterpreted our responsibility for the land because we have misunderstood our own purpose in being on the land; we have misinterpreted our call to dominate and subdue as a freedom rather than a responsibility to imitate God.

What, therefore, is the underlying purpose of this land? Why is this land here? Why is this earth here? Certainly to provide all the basic needs of the critters, human or otherwise, that dwell on it. But there again our thinking is utilitarian. Beneath and undergirding this provision of substance is the reminder of its source: the purpose of the land is to point to its Creator; to draw our hearts in gratitude upward; to see God's hand and creative will in every hill and valley, every plant, every creature. If we see only through utilitarian eyes, vegetation becomes graded into plants and weeds, useful and useless; animals are divided into livestock and vermin, useful and useless; and dare I remind the reader that throughout history, man has done the same with man? Yet even the supposedly useless—mosquitoes, leeches, spiders, snakes, rats, and vultures—all have their place in God's creation and show the amazing intricacy of His miraculous and providential creativity.

Before attacking any piece of land with bulldozer, brush hog, or plow, I would suggest taking a chair and sitting for a while in the seemingly unproductive wilderness. Relax before a bursting hedge of intertwined wildflowers, "weeds", briars, and scrub trees, and patiently observe the shapes, colors, and textures of the leaves, flowers, twigs, stems, soil, and rocks; the occasional insect and bird; the footprints of wildlife in the dirt; the sounds; and the wind. These are the "vestiges" that Saint Bonaventure spoke of in his *Journey of the Mind to God*. All of this is God's "still small voice" (1 Kings 19:12) that reminds us that before we consider the land's utilitarian value, we must, in awe and gratefulness, recognize the land as a sign of His creative love. By beginning here, we are freed from the guilt-producing utilitarian *should*s that insist that unless we make our land productive, self-sustaining, or profitable, we have failed before God in our stewardship. Instead, we discover that, unless a more utilitarian purpose is clearly necessary— say, to provide needed food or profit for our family—we are free to enjoy and use the land in whatever way we believe gives honor to its Creator. Since my family's present situation does not demand that I provide food or profit from the land, I'm essentially free to let the land

once again go fallow. I could choose to spend the rest of my days watching the land return to wilderness from grass to briars to scrub trees to hardwoods, and also watch the wildlife return, possibly in abundance. Or, I can even choose to turn some acreage into the Richard Crown Memorial Softball Field.

Yet, I am also free to study the land, its traits and characteristics, to determine the most appropriate ways to develop this land for food, profit, or pleasure—as long as whatever I do does not run counter to its intended purpose: to give glory to God and draw our hearts upward in gratitude.

Like every piece of land, each man is different, with a unique combination of gifts, experiences, history, training, and opportunities. Each is called to be a good steward of this life and the unique talents we have been given. The problem is, from the time most of us reached the age when the question of work made any sense to our childhood brains, we were being graded through utilitarian eyes. Would we grow to become productive components in our society? Were we good students, per the criteria of our modern educational system? What college would we attend? What major and what career?

How many of us were directed down vocational paths by people who might have been trying to fulfill their own dreams vicariously through us? How many of us have been discouraged from thinking we had any meaningful purpose in living, anything of importance to share or do, by people who themselves were discouraged and bitter about life? How many of us have been convinced that life itself has no meaning or purpose by people who themselves have no clue about the meaning of life—who passed along their own sense of being lost to us like an infected person passing along a disease? And how many of us have been convinced by our materialistic culture that the only definable purpose for anyone's life is to get a job that can make the most money; that college and career are the only pathways to success, meaning, and happiness? What about those people, numbering possibly into the millions, who are not college bound, who have neither the means nor the opportunities to land a promising lucrative career? Are they to see themselves as losers, as "lesser-thans," as people for whom God had no meaningful purpose other than as pawns in the bigger games played by those intended, from the beginning of time, to be the true players in the game of life?

Scripture teaches consistently that God has purposely created, knows, and loves each and every person, of every culture, on every continent. This is particularly proclaimed by the psalmist: "For you formed my inward parts, you knitted me together in my mother's womb.... Your eyes beheld my unformed substance; in your book were written, every one of them, the days that were formed for me, when as yet there was none of them" (Ps 139:13, 16). In a certain yet mysterious way, each of us was planted from birth into a unique circumstance with unique opportunities and gifts, our own unique biology and environment, nature and nurture, all bound together with that unique character of soul; and in the mystery of God's love, to temper, test, and mature these gifts, we were each allotted unique challenges—handicaps, if you will. For some, these challenges involve biological or environmental encumbrances, sometimes seemingly insurmountable; for others, these challenges are a seeming overabundance of blessings, beauty, opportunities, riches, and talents. In whatever case, each of us is given these challenges to help us become the persons we were created to be. As Saint Paul wrote, "[W]e rejoice in our sufferings, knowing that suffering produces endurance, and endurance produces character, and character produces hope, and hope does not disappoint us, because God's love has been poured into our hearts through the Holy Spirit who has been given to us" (Rom 5:3–5).

If we look at ourselves and those around us primarily through utilitarian eyes, however, none of this works. The majority of the world's population becomes graded as useless and unproductive; men and women, boys and girls with even the slightest handicap become mere burdens, and only the beautiful, the wealthy, the gifted, and the educated are deemed worthy. The Nazi doctors took this to the extreme, but lest we point fingers, Americans used eugenics in the early twentieth century to prevent the unproductive from polluting the gene pool—and our modern industrial capitalistic system was built on and is still driven by these assumptions.

This is why, as when appraising a piece of land, we must begin with the initial question: For what purpose has each person been created? Here we reach that ultimate question: "Why are we here?" Rather than press this question from every angle, which would require a much larger book and an author with a far higher pay grade, I'll pass along what I consider a most beautiful answer, for no one says it better than Saint Ignatius of Loyola:

> God freely created us so that we might know, love, and serve him in this life and be happy with him forever. God's purpose in creating us is to draw forth from us a response of love and service here on earth, so that we may attain our goal of everlasting happiness with him in heaven.[1]

This is a purpose that is attainable for every single person in the world, regardless of class, color, culture, education, or economics. Certainly, situations render this more or less accessible to individuals or groups, yet this is why God calls us to recognize our communal responsibilities. We are called to take care of and share with our brothers and sisters all the resources we have received from God through His creation. Saint Ignatius confirms this in the continuation of the above statement:

[1] Ignatius of Loyola, *The Spiritual Exercises* in David L. Fleming, S.J., *Draw Me Into Your Friendship: A Literal Translation and a Contemporary Reading of the Spiritual Exercises* (St. Louis, Mo.: Institute of Jesuit Sources, 1996).

All the things in this world are gifts of God, created for us, to be the means by which we can come to know him better, love him more surely, and serve him more faithfully. As a result, we ought to appreciate and use these gifts of God insofar as they help us toward our goal of loving service and union with God. But insofar as any created things hinder our progress toward our goal, we ought to let them go.[2]

So, what is the best use of our lives? How do we weed through the myriad of opinions inundating us from every conceivable direction, to discern what is the intended goal for our lives? Well, to a certain extent, unless God has made definitively clear His unique specific calling for our lives, as He did with Moses, Abraham, John the Baptist, Saint Paul, and hundreds of others throughout history, we are free to do whatever we please—as long as it fulfills and does not contradict our deeper purpose. Situations may limit our freedom to choose certain options, yet we each have the option of accepting our situations as somehow within the mysterious plan of God. As Saint Paul confessed, "Not that I complain of want; for I have learned, in whatever state I am, to be content" (Phil 4:11). By examining the unique quiver of talents, opportunities, and challenges we each have been given, we can discern ways in which we might best build on these gifts—and for land, this means examining the soil.

Stages of Soil

So, the question arose: What kind of soil has God given us on this land? What's it good for? The soil survey map published by the U.S. Department of Agriculture indicates that our small chunk of Muskingum County consists of contours of Westmoreland-Guernsey silt loans, eroded soil of slopes varying from 8 to 40 percent sloped eroded soil. The report states that, though our land is blessed with good drainage (i.e., no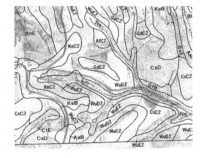

chance of floods), "these soils are poorly suited to cultivated crops
... [and] ... only moderately suited for hay and pasture ... and timber production."[3] The bottom line is that we have been blessed with
some of the least fertile and usable land in our county. We therefore
were faced with a dilemma.

Examining the varieties of soil that make up our land, especially
discovering that they are far from fruitful, reminded me of maybe
the most familiar agrarian parable that Jesus told His mostly agrarian audience: that of the sower, as given in Matthew 13. Traditionally, this has been understood to describe four different ways that
people receive the gospel message: the first three soils represent people who receive it inadequately and fall away, unfruitful, while the
fourth "good soil" represents those who hear the Word, understand
it, and consequently bear fruit (Mt 13:23).

Over the years, I've met people at every point along the spiritual
spectrum, from being completely alienated from God to being almost
in rapturous union with Him. With the desire to help the alienated
ones come closer to rapturous union, I've often preached on this parable: "Which kind of soil are you? What rocks or weeds pollute your
life and rob you of the nourishment of God's Word?"

Then, as I heard the parable once again recently, reflecting
especially on the journeys of those I've interviewed on my television program, it struck me that Jesus was referring not only to
four kinds of people but also to four stages of the spiritual journey
through which many of us pass. For example, in verse 19, Jesus
described, "When any one hears the word of the kingdom and does
not understand it, the Evil One comes and snatches away what is
sown in his heart." This sounds like what happened to so many of
us who "heard" the faith when we were quite young, in Sunday
school or Confirmation class, for instance, but didn't understand it.
Good, faithful teachers and preachers planted it in our hearts, but
soon enough the Evil One snatched it away, or at least turned our
attention away from that which remained planted deep within. As
a result, far more interested in other, more worldly matters, many

[3] Soil Survey of Muskingum County, Ohio (National Cooperative Soil Survey, a joint
effort of the United States Department of Agriculture and other federal agencies, issued June
1996), 119.

of us walked away from the faith. Does this sound familiar, in your own life or in the life of someone close to you?

Then, in verses 20 and 21, Jesus said, "As for what was sown on rocky ground, this is he who hears the word and immediately receives it with joy; yet he has no root in himself, but endures for a while, and when tribulation or persecution arises on account of the word, immediately he falls away." This sounds like what happens to many of us during our young adult years. Without yet any burdensome responsibilities (such as marriage, family, or work) and with far too much freedom, many respond with enthusiastic joy to charismatic preachers or winsome Bible teachers, and, with great emotions, come back to church. Over time, though, the "rocks" of our relativistic, narcissistic, ambition-driven culture can get in the way, preventing our faith from deepening and robbing us of "the joy of salvation" (see Ps 51:12). As life becomes complicated and challenges to our rediscovered faith arise, we drift back into a nominal minimalism.

Then in verse 22, Jesus continued: "As for what was sown among thorns, this is he who hears the word, but the cares of the world and the delight in riches choke the word, and it proves unfruitful." This sounds like what happens to many of us later in our adult years: as we become increasingly successful in business, prosperous, and popular, the voice of the Word becomes squelched and silenced within our minds. And just like the thorns in the parable, trusting in the promises of our modern economic empire can choke us out of true, everlasting hope. We may have made efforts in the past to weed the demons of sin and immoral habits out of our lives, only to fail by letting them return, maybe sevenfold (see Mt 12:43–45), out of neglect, sloth, and complacent pride.

But then Jesus spoke of the fourth soil. Here he addressed that point in many people's lives, whether they are young, middle-aged, or in their waning years, when by the merciful grace of God, they not only *hear* but *understand* the gospel. Or, as Saint Luke has it, "they are those who, hearing the word, hold it fast in an honest and good heart, and bring forth fruit with patience" (Lk 8:15). This occurs when we shamefacedly recognize our self-centered sinfulness and the truth that any of the things that, since childhood, have choked the faith out of us did so only with our consent. This fourth soil of conversion represents that point in our lives when, by grace, we humbly come back to God with gratitude, like the prodigal son into the arms of the Father.

Looking at our land was like looking at my own soul. The fields were in a variety of stages of development, representing all four of the soils that Jesus mentioned, and more. Everywhere from boundary to boundary, the soil was embedded with rocks, mostly flint, and the dormant seeds of weeds, briars, brambles, and thorns all awaiting the opportunity to sprout and take over the property. Given the many times I myself have started with enthusiasm but failed to purge my life of the sins and vices that held me back from intimate union with Christ, I could have given up purging this land of its weeds before even starting. But I remembered another important agrarian image our Lord used to encourage His followers to trust that, with Him, anything is possible: "Come to me, all who labor and are heavy laden, and I will give you rest. *Take my yoke upon you*, and learn from me; for I am gentle and lowly in heart, and you will find rest for your souls. For my yoke is easy, and my burden is light" (Mt 11:28–30, emphasis mine). One of the biggest problems of farming—mega, large, small, or hobby—today is the absence of farming neighbors and the shortage of willing and affordable labor. I remember once hearing a poem entitled something like "For Want of a Third Hand", about the trials of doing farm work alone. In the past, farming neighbors made farming possible, as they shared and helped—as they shouldered together the yoke of each other's responsibilities. In this scriptural promise, our Lord invites us to partner with Him to face anything that life brings our way.

If we look at the world only through secular eyes, we see only what we humans can accomplish, alone, together, or at each other's throats, as we have been for most of history—or, only blaming mankind for what we have done to damage "Mother Earth." If, however, we look at the world through the eyes of faith, the light of Christ can disperse the clouds of discouragement and fear to reveal a horizon of limitless hope, to help us not only *hear* His Word of hope but *understand* it, so that our lives, wherever He has planted us, can "bring forth fruit with patience". With His help, we can recognize and manage the stewardship of our portion of God's creation.

Setting Boundaries

After studying the soil—and rediscovering why this part of Ohio is known for its fire-kilned clay pottery—Marilyn and I needed to consider other factors to determine the best use of this particular land. From the opinions of neighbors and myr- iad books, it appeared that the best use of our hilly land, besides maybe for lumber, firewood, and the occasional attack of a brush-hog mower, was for the grazing of sheep or cattle. For this, the fields needed perimeter fences, which were present but in desperate need of repair. In fact, nearly a quarter mile of the southern fence line was a sieve, consisting of hilly terrain and a meandering creek, fallen or rotten trees, briars, poison ivy, and a deteriorating woven fence that had been patched dozens of times with strands of rusted barbwire. After several years of our hand clearing, brush hogging, and bulldoz-ing, and with a completely new high-tensile electric fence, the field eventually was reclaimed and the fence was ready to bounce back any wandering livestock or hungry predators, which in our area are stray dogs or coyotes. Then with the addition of a dozen sheep, the rejuvenated pasture was a beautiful sight.

As I indicated before, I'm possibly the worst farmer ever, so after a season and a host of reasons, our flock had dwindled to six, and these ended up at the auction barn. For a year the field sat, until we were ready to try our hand at feeder calves. The fence lines, however, had become so overgrown that we couldn't turn on the electric—the fields could not be used for their intended purpose. So my sons and I spent a weekend clearing and string trimming, repairing one section where a hollow tree full of bees had fallen and temporarily knocked down the wires. When evening came, we once again saw a clear fence line, which actually was better than it had ever been before.

Boundaries are important and must be constantly tended, especially when it comes to our spiritual lives. It has long been said that the eye is the door to the soul. The great spiritual writers, philosophers, and theologians have long recognized that we are not merely souls trapped in physical bodies, as if salvation comes through freedom from this earthly shell. Rather, we are unified persons, body and soul, which was expressed through the Incarnation and Resurrection of Jesus Christ. When we profess in the Creed, "I believe in the resurrection of the body", we mean that for eternity we will exist as a unified person, with a resurrected body and soul. All this to say that what we do with our bodies, what we allow to enter us through our senses—what we see, hear, taste, smell, and feel—affects us, heart, mind, and soul, and therefore our entire person.

I suppose a farm analogy of this, though truly imperfect, is that what our cow eats directly affects the taste and quality of her milk. If she has grazed in a patch of wild onions or skunk cabbage, you know it when you pour her milk on your cereal! It's also true that what she eats greatly affects the taste and texture of her meat after she ends up in the freezer. The lean meat of purely grass-fed beef has a radically different taste (at least to me) from the meat of at least partially grain-fed beef. This is why we must provide strong boundaries to keep the cow away from what is bad for her so she can feed on what is good.

Such is true for the spiritual health of our entire being. Boundaries to our senses, boundaries to what we put into our body, protect more than just our girth or our attitudes; they protect and form our conscience, our soul, our entire being. Allow your boundaries to slip into disrepair, and before you know it, you may become a different, unrecognizable person, outside and in.

Spiritual Entropy

It is truly amazing how quickly this land can return to its native state if not tended carefully. A substantial portion of our twenty-five acres had been left fallow for nearly thirty years. As a result, it had completely returned to scrub forest intermixed with briars.

This reminded me of another parable, which shows our Lord truly knew His agrarian audience—and it made me wonder whether it was even worth starting to clear and improve this land:

> When the unclean spirit has gone out of a man, he passes through waterless places seeking rest; and finding none he says, "I will return to my house from which I came." And when he comes he finds it swept and put in order. Then he goes and brings seven other spirits more evil than himself, and they enter and dwell there; and the last state of that man becomes worse than the first. (Lk 11:24–26)

It takes more than a tremendous amount of time and effort; it takes a good dose of God-given talent, knowledge, patience, and partnership with willing helpers to "weed" a piece of land so that it can be reaped. But once the land has been purged of weeds, "swept and put in order", the job isn't done, for after a season or two of neglect, those demon weeds, briars, brambles, thorns, and first-growth junk trees will return sevenfold, "more evil" than what has been removed, "and the last state of that [land] becomes worse than the first."

Given my city-slicker inexperience, I hired a man to clear the worst section of the acreage down to bare dirt, pushing all the junk trees and brambles into a pile for burning. I had hoped to replant with pasture grass, but my busyness got in the way. Within a year, that bare land had completely grown back with over-the-shoulder-high grasses, briars, and weeds.

This is a natural example of *entropy*, which the *Merriam-Webster Dictionary* defines as "the degradation of the matter and energy in the universe to an ultimate state of inert uniformity". More simply, entropy measures the usual movement in nature of order to disorder. Without the input of energy to establish and maintain order, everything in nature moves toward disorder (and this can be scientifically proven by looking into any adult male's sock drawer).

This is also a God-given illustration of "spiritual entropy". If we neglect to take time to examine the state of our soul, to repent, pray, worship, meditate on God's Word, and love, this neglect will become the state of our soul. As the great Dominican theologian Reginald Garrigou-Lagrange once said, "In the way of God, he who makes no progress loses ground."[4] We never in this life reach a safe plateau where we can presume we have spiritually arrived. If we are not growing in our relationship with God the Father through His Son, Jesus Christ, by the power of the Holy Spirit, we are dying—we are losing ground. Saint Paul's letter to the Ephesians is all about this. Paul was writing to Christians who had been saved by grace through faith from their former pagan way of life (see 2:8). He exhorted them to continue, even though "saved", to "[p]ut off the old man which belongs to your former manner of life and is corrupt through deceitful lusts, and be renewed in the spirit of your minds, and put on the new man, created after the likeness of God in true righteousness and holiness" (4:22–24).

I remember hearing a story about a tourist driving across Scotland, admiring the rolling farmlands, until one particularly beautiful and abundant garden stopped him in his tracks. He got out of his car to admire the well-kept and bountiful rows of vegetables. As he approached, the Scottish gardener suddenly popped up into view from behind an enormous berry bush. The tourist exclaimed, "My, God has blessed you with a beautiful garden!" To that, the Scottish gardener replied, "Ach! You shoulda seen it when God had it to His lonesome!"

Without the willful input of energy and effort through the aid of grace, our spiritual lives can quickly move from order to disorder.

By grace, we generally do not regress spiritually all the way back to our "former manner of life"—that is, if we regularly reexamine the purpose, the quality of soil, the boundaries, and the order in our lives. If we have forgotten or never taken the time to consider the reason God created us and placed us in this world, if we have neglected the nurturing of our mind and heart, if we have become negligent in maintaining adequate boundaries around our senses and person, and therefore our conscience and soul, we likely have allowed our lives to drift into seemingly paralyzing disorder. We can, nonetheless, clear-cut the weeds, brambles, and junk trees from our lives; we can reestablish the boundaries; we can reestablish order; and we can remember and recommit ourselves to the very purpose for which

---

[4] Reginald Garrigou-Lagrange, O.P., *The Three Ways of the Spiritual Life* (Rockford, Ill.: TAN Books, 1977), 30.

we were created. All it takes is contrition, repentance, and recommitment to Him who knew each of us before we were even formed in the womb. All of this is possible through prayer and the graces God gives us.

Just as I cannot expect the condition of my land to be preserved without effort, we must never presume upon our past or present relationship with God, for "on this side of heaven" there is always the possibility that we can drift away and lose it all (see Heb 6:4ff), for "[y]our adversary the devil prowls around like a roaring lion, seeking some one to devour" (1 Pet 5:8). Fulfilling our purpose and living an ordered life within faithful boundaries require that we not expect God to do it all on "His lonesome". At the same time we must remember His warning that apart from Him we can do nothing (see Jn 15:5) but with Him all things are possible (see Mk 10:27).

4

Conserving Fire

And I will put my Spirit within you, and you shall live,
and I will place you in your own land;
then you shall know that I, the LORD, have spoken,
and I have done it, says the LORD.

—Ezekiel 37:14

My three sons and I love to make bonfires. Our small piece of land, far from efficiently developed, is strewn with dead trees and brush—especially after having timber removed from our woods last year, leaving over a hundred treetops waiting to be harvested for firewood. The boys and I could make a bonfire a month for the rest of our lives and still not conquer the chaos.

During one such conflagration, it struck me how little mankind has progressed in being a faithful steward of one of the greatest gifts God has given us: fire. Man has indeed developed an amazing array of technologies—all of which, of course, come from God: man has created nothing but only developed what Providence has revealed to us. We still, though, have only inefficiently utilized this most primitive of gifts.

There before me was a spectacular thermal reaction: otherwise worthless dead natural wood, briars, and leaves were being transformed into brilliant light and intense heat. On this particular occasion, the heat was so unbearable that my son Richard and I had to whittle ten-foot hickory limbs into hot dog skewers, rather than using the usual six-foot spicebush branches.

As I reflected, with our dog, Bungie, at my side, it occurred to me: we live in a modern age of previously unimaginable technologies, where far too many of the world's conflicts are over who has control of the energy to power these technologies, yet there, right before me, was the most primitive of technologies—fire—and we have not discovered how to save and use this energy efficiently, particularly here in my own backyard. Certainly, on a larger scale, we can put a closed vessel of water over fire to produce steam that can turn a fan to drive a turbine to produce electricity that can power a lightbulb or a furnace, but think of how inefficient this is: many indirect steps are necessary to turn light and heat into light and heat—and in fact the original light produced by the fire isn't even used. Scientists are presently working with silicon nanowire technology in an attempt to shorten the transference, but despite all we have accomplished and are discovering, we are still a long way from conserving and using directly the heat and light energy of a basic backyard bonfire.

This reflection led me to consider how inefficient we are as stewards of the fires of our own souls. There is nothing so powerful in the universe as a soul that has been changed by grace, from a lackluster, cold, self-absorbed sinner into an enthusiastic, enlightened, empowered, on-fire, yet humble child of God. When this happens, either as the result of a long, slow, grace-filled process beginning with baptism or of a grace-sparked explosion, God has nonetheless changed us, from the inside out. As Saint Paul wrote, "[I]f any one is in Christ, he is a new creation; the old has passed away, behold, the new has come" (2 Cor 5:17). In words similar to those of Christ when He spoke of being born anew through "water and the Spirit" (i.e., baptism; cf. Jn 3:3–5), Saint Peter described this transformation: "By his great mercy we have been born anew to a living hope through the resurrection of Jesus Christ from the dead ... not of perishable seed but of imperishable, through the living and abiding word of God" (1 Pet 1:3, 23).

Even more boldly, Saint Peter further proclaimed that by this rebirth, we have "become partakers of the divine nature" (2 Pet 1:4). We may not feel any different, for this indwelling of God's divine nature, the Holy Spirit, this fire of grace, is an imperceptible fire in the deep boiler room of our soul. The heat and light of this inner fire, however, can and do emerge, kindling our heart and our mind, empowering our emotions, our intellect, and our will, radiating from our eyes, our hands, and our words. And whatever fire has been ignited by grace in our innermost being is not only for our own well-being and salvation but primarily for the enlightenment and salvation of others.

On the morning after our latest bonfire, all that was left was a large gray circle of ashes. We had enjoyed the light and the heat for a brief time, but afterward all that was left were spent coals. Frankly, far too many of us are like that spent fire. Many of us have squandered the inner fire of our baptism, ignoring or rejecting this inner gift of grace, or even progressing through life oblivious to this gift that we were given long ago through the generosity of our parents, who brought us forward and presented us in faith to God. Many of us, not seeing the expected effects of this supposed inner fire in the lives of others—ministers, priests, bishops, deacons, religious, and laity who show few visible signs of inner conversion—have turned away from the faith, opting for a naturalistic view of life.

This is contrary to Jesus' intention. He wanted far more than a mere forest fire of evangelization; He desired the entire world to be set on fire: "I came to cast fire upon the earth; and would that it were already kindled!" (Lk 12:49). There are certainly places where the Smokey Bear mentality makes sense, but not when it comes to kindling the flame of God's presence in our soul or the fulfillment of Christ's Great Commission (see Mt 28:18–20). Saint Paul warned the early Christians of this danger when he exhorted them: "Do not quench the Spirit" (1 Thess 5:19).

So what can we do to rekindle this inner flame and to ensure that the heat and light of the indwelling divine nature of the Spirit are not squandered? I wish I could give an easy answer, just as I wish I could invent the technology to power my home from my backyard bonfires. As a lowly individual, outside the powerful technological industrial stream, I can't expect to solve the big energy questions nor waste my life waiting. In the meantime, I can (1) appreciate and enjoy the heat and light of my backyard bonfires, (2) share this with my family and friends, and (3) look for other ways to utilize this God-given free source of heat and light—in the deep cold winter, my family and I are able to bring that bonfire into our wood-burning stove, heat our entire home, and enjoy popcorn by the fire's light.

In the same way, each one of us, recognizing the gift of this inner transforming grace, can begin right now with these same three resolutions.

Appreciate the Heat and Light of God's Love

First, Saint Paul told us precisely how to keep from "quenching the Spirit": "Rejoice always, pray constantly, give thanks in all circumstances; for this is the will of God" (1 Thess 5:16–18). These are the necessary attitudes that make our mind, heart, and soul receptive to the rekindling and flaring up of that inner fire.

We begin by pausing to appreciate with humble gratitude the grace and enlightenment we have received from the Father. We may not remember having had a specific, powerfully ecstatic religious experience—God in His wisdom does not seem to think that this is best for everyone; maybe only the weak ones (like me) need this. However, if you love God and desire to grow closer to Him and to experience the heat and light of this inner fire, this proves that you have been touched by His grace—otherwise you would not care! Stop, even right now, and enjoy the heat and light of His presence in your life, in your heart and soul, and thank Him for His mercy.

Share the Fire

Second, consider ways to share what you have been given within the immediate "mission field" where you have been planted: among your family, friends, and coworkers. What you have been given by God may be but the tip of an iceberg of renewal. Certainly the voices of the world, the flesh, and the devil will try to discourage you from opening your mouth or your hands. But really, it's just as simple as looking for an opportunity to share the light and heat you have been given with those around you—not from above them, as if our religious experiences make us somehow special, but from beside them. We can ask God to help us see how we can help others "rekindle the gift of God that is within" each of us, through our baptism, our surrender in faith, our confirmation, and "the laying on of ... hands". As Saint Paul told Saint Timothy, "God did not give us a spirit of timidity but a spirit of power and love and self-control" (2 Tim 1:6, 7).

"Power ... love ... self-control." These sound like forms of God-given energy that we can always look for ways to help each other conserve and implement. Maybe some night while sitting around a campfire, watching the embers float upward into the dark blue sky, we can tap into this hidden "spirit of power and love and self-control" and help those around us recognize the fingerprints of the Creator in everything around us. We might even boldly say, almost like telling a story, "Can I tell you about the most important person in my life?" and tell them about how Jesus Christ has changed our lives through that indwelling fire.

Find New Ways to Use His Fire

And third, prayerfully ask God to help you see how He might be calling you to act on the gifts of heat and light in your soul to change the lives of those around you in your community. How can you help the Church at the local or wider level to spread the heat and light of Jesus Christ to a culture and nation that so desperately need Him?

Many of us might feel that there are no embers left inside; that whatever inner fire there might have been long ago has been quenched, leaving only the remnants of ashes and unconsumed dreams. Appearances, however, can be deceiving. As I mentioned earlier, my family and I are able to heat our home with a small wood-burning stove. This takes a lot of prep work months beforehand—cutting, splitting, transporting, and stacking wood—as well as vigilance, stoking and restoking the stove all day and sometimes all night long. In the first winters of our life on our rural property, it seemed that every morning we had to rebuild the fire from scratch, removing the ashes, wadding newspaper, splitting logs into fine kindling, and then trying two, three times until the fire was once again burning on its own. Because this routine was at times laborious, we often just gave up on the wood burner and let the gas furnace take over and burn propane at will.

This past winter, though, we decided to be better stewards of what God has given us: acres of trees and cords upon cords of downed trunks and limbs just waiting to be used for their intended purpose—as opposed to our surrendering to the burning of more propane while letting the natural heat sources rot. I guess this is a form of subsidiarity: using the gifts nearest to us, rather than stepping over these to send our money far away into some unknown person's pocket.

In the process of being more vigilant, we discovered something that all experienced homesteaders already know. Now, in the morning, with the coffee brewing, I open the woodstove to find the grate covered an inch deep in ash. It looks hopeless. But using the iron fire poker, I move the ashes around so they sift down through the grate into the removable ashbin. In the process, red-hot coals appear. Once the ashes are all in the bin, I load three logs into the fire chamber on top of the coals, close the doors, and then open the bottom ashbin drawer to remove it for emptying, leaving the grate floor of the fire chamber open. In the time it takes me to carry the ashbin outside, empty it, and return it to the stove, the air whooshing up through the open grate has so rekindled those seemingly spent coals that the three logs have become a brilliant and formidable blaze. We now go days on end without needing to relight from scratch; we just uncover and rekindle the coals each morning.

Regardless of how spiritually spent you might feel—or how long it has been since you paid any attention to God or His Church, His Word, His sacraments, or His love—if you desire to return to God, the existence of this *desire* is the evidence that you still have within you, hidden beneath the ashes of years of neglect, failures, and self-indulgence, the coals of His divine nature received long ago in baptism. Even if you were never baptized, but once long ago accepted Him by faith, He is still there, within your soul, for He promised that

He would never forsake us. And even if you have never previously expressed any interest in God, yet now sense a desire to know Him, the very existence of this *desire* is the evidence of His grace working within your heart.

As I mentioned earlier, we can rekindle the long-neglected coals of God's inner presence by stopping, even right now, to rejoice in Him, to thank Him in whatever circumstances for His constant love, to ask forgiveness for our long neglect and rebellion, and through a return to the sacraments, to enjoy the fire and light of His presence in our lives. All it takes is to acknowledge with the psalmist: "The LORD is my light and my salvation; whom shall I fear?" (27:1).

Lord, help us, for living all around each of us are people in need of the heat and light of Your love. May they not go without because we have not taken the time to share.

5

Graceberries

Since we have these promises, beloved, let us cleanse our-
selves from every defilement of body and spirit, and make
holiness perfect in the fear of God.

—2 Corinthians 7:1

When the warmth and long sun of midsummer hits, nearly every day finds at least one member of my family fighting through the briar patches, protected by long-sleeved sweaty shirts and jeans, toting those modern plastic coffee containers with handles, in an effort to harvest our main crop: wild raspberries and blackberries. We also call these delicious morsels "graceberries" because they appear just like magic on our land. We did nothing to cause them to happen—especially nothing to  deserve them. In fact, the less we do to clear away the brambles, the seemingly more plump and luscious the berries become every year. I'm sure this isn't true—and just a quick glance at any gardening book would probably instruct me to trim away the deadwood and cut back the growth annually. But so far, our limited input has not seemed to limit the output.

The *Catechism* defines *grace* as *"favor, the free and undeserved help* that God gives us to respond to his call to become children of God,

adoptive sons, partakers of the divine nature and of eternal life."[1] It
then expounds on this:

> Grace is a *participation in the life of God*. It introduces us into the inti-
> macy of Trinitarian life: by Baptism the Christian participates in
> the grace of Christ, the Head of his Body. As an "adopted son" he
> can henceforth call God "Father," in union with the only Son. He
> receives the life of the Spirit who breathes charity into him and who
> forms the Church.[2]

God's undeserved grace is freely given, and for a purpose, and that
grace requires our acceptance and willful actualization. Grace can be
squandered—as can our freely given, undeserved wild raspberries,
which likewise are given for a purpose and require our acceptance
and willful actualization.

Several years ago, due to other commitments and entanglements,
we were unable to pick any berries. They nevertheless ignored our
irresponsibility and turned lusciously black and juicy just the same.
Some of them were enjoyed by our welcome guests—the birds, the
deer, and our dogs—and our less-than-welcome guests—the bugs—
but the residual berries all rotted, hardened, and remained as visual
reminders of squandered grace.

We've learned from experience that picking the berries as soon
as they turn black allows the plant's nutrition to flow more freely
into the remaining berries, initiating more growth. Sometimes it
seems as if just turning around causes more berries to pop! As long as
it's berry season, we can return to the same plants day after day and
find new ripe graceberries.

Growing by grace in holiness is like that: acting on grace to eradicate sin and vice initiates the growth of virtue; ignoring or failing to
act on grace opens the door to vice and squelches virtue.

As I worked my way through the briars early one evening, some
lessons from berry picking began to ripen.

---

[1] *Catechism of the Catholic Church (CCC)*, 2nd ed. (Vatican City: Libreria Editrice Vaticana,
2000), no. 1996 (emphasis in original). Cf. Jn 1:12–18; 17:3; Rom 8:14–17; 2 Pet 1:3–4.
[2] *CCC*, no. 1997.

"Suffering Produces Endurance"—and Welts!

Invariably the largest, most luscious berries are deep within the brambles, and those prickly branches hurt! The way they attack, you'd think there were little demons in those bushes. The minute I'd stretch deep into a bush to pluck a few little fruits, two or three thorn-laden branches would wrap themselves around my back, locking me in until rescuers could arrive. I'm no biblical scholar, but I'm sure that God must have added the prickly spikes *after* the fall of Adam and Eve.

Those little thorns are reminiscent of Saint Paul's teaching in Romans that, though we are heirs of Christ, this privilege comes "provided we suffer with him in order that we may also be glorified with him" (8:17). As it is with harvesting bramble berries, so it is in our spiritual lives as well: the greatest blessings always come with some suffering or sacrifice. Suffering also produces the "endurance" and "character" (Rom 5:3, 4) we need, so that one day we may, by grace, hear those important words, "Well done, good and faithful servant" (Mt 25:21).

"Bring Forth Fruit with Patience"

The greatest blessings always require patience. As the psalmist said, "Be still before the LORD, and wait patiently for him; ... those who wait for the LORD shall possess the land" (37:7, 9). Those who pick berries in a hurry—only to get it done quickly so they can move on to something else—will invariably have three times the number of prickle pricks and a third the number of good berries. Or more likely, no berries at all, since they usually get spilled if the picker runs home (just ask my sons).

If we relax and take the time to delight carefully in the God-given privilege and beauty found in picking each berry (or any other task He gives us), the overall experience is always more rewarding. So goes the advice of the psalmist: "Take delight in the LORD, and he will give you the desires of your heart" (37:4).

Thorns and Stumbling Blocks

We must never be so quickly convinced that we've picked the bushes clean. Whenever my family and I begin picking, we generally pick the easy-to-reach berries first. Then with these branches seemingly picked bare, we initially declare our work complete, but from experience we know there's always more. So we fight the good fight into and through the shoulder-high bramble patch, only to discover dozens of additional luscious berries taunting us in plain view. From our original perspective, they were hidden behind leaves, but now from a new angle, they are blatantly manifest.

So it is with sin and bad habits. We must not stop after we've cleansed ourselves of our obvious sins but must dig deeper and look at ourselves from a fresh angle—from the perspective of our suffering Savior, as Saint Paul did (see Phil 3:7–16)—and then we'll see that not one of us has yet reached perfection.

One evening, as I worked my way in and through those dense bushes, my foot hit something hard and nearly sent me cartwheeling down the hill into the creek. When I pushed the weeds and thorns aside to see what it was, I found an old granite foundation stone that I had discovered years before and had intended to get help to move. Instead, I had put it off and forgotten all about it.

Sin is that way, of course, and the more we put it off, the more overgrown it becomes, until it eventually becomes just another part of our lives, our character. We can become so accustomed to sin that we grow blind to its presence and effects, and the greatest of these blind sins is pride—the stubborn insistence that we have no need to change. Pride can convince us, like the impatient berry picker, that we don't need to grow any more or dig any deeper to eradicate vices, if this requires suffering or sacrifice, and especially if a vice has become a long-standing, well-entrenched habit or even a hallmark of our character—in other words, if it would demand too much self-effacement to admit fault and try to change.

But it is essential that we eradicate pride and the many other thorns that prevent us from being fruitful—from growing in grace. If we allow sin to remain, like that long-forgotten granite stone, it will cause us to obey our passions, rather than our consciences (see Rom 6:12–13).

Cutting Away Dead Wood

In one of his greatest agrarian images, our Lord warned, "I am the true vine, and my Father is the vinedresser. Every branch of mine that bears no fruit, he takes away, and every branch that does bear fruit he prunes, that it may bear more fruit" (Jn 15:1–2). Over the years, I have discovered and reluctantly admitted something that all good horticulturalists instinctively know: that I can indeed increase as well as improve the quality of our berry harvest if, months before the flowers and buds appear, I take the time to prune our many berry patches, cutting away unproductive dead canes, snipping back over-grown canes, and clearing a path around and through each patch to make more of the fruit accessible.

In our lives, our Lord prunes away our dead canes through suffering and sacramental confession. In the following long quote from the First Letter of John, we hear a clear expression of why and how the pruning must be done:

> If we say we have fellowship with him while we walk in darkness, we lie and do not live according to the truth; but if we walk in the light, as he is in the light, we have fellowship with one another, and the blood of Jesus his Son cleanses us from all sin. If we say we have no sin, we deceive ourselves, and the truth is not in us. If we confess our sins, he is faithful and just, and will forgive our sins and cleanse us from all unrighteousness. If we say we have not sinned, we make him a liar, and his word is not in us. (1:6–10)

Very serious stuff. A poorly bearing berry bush overgrown with dead, unproductive canes eventually is "cast forth as a branch and withers; and the branches are gathered, thrown into the fire and burned" (Jn 15:6)—and so accumulates the tinder for our many bonfires. This is what Jesus says sin does to us: it robs us of the fruit of virtue, righteousness, and goodness. We can be cleansed of these thorns, however, through the graces of confession. Jesus gave this lifesaving authority to His Church after His Resurrection: "Jesus said to them again, 'Peace be with you. As the Father has sent me, even so I send you.' And when he had said this, he breathed on them, and said to them, 'Receive the Holy Spirit. If you forgive the sins of any, they are forgiven; if you retain the sins of any, they are retained'" (Jn 20:21–23).

God—who "desires all men to be saved and to come to the knowledge of the truth" (1 Tim 2:4)—in His infinite mercy and love can use any means, any situation to grant the free gift of His divine life. He gives this gift to all with the design to move them to seek Him with a sincere heart.[3] This requires that we fight through the briars of doubt, discouragement, pride, and self-sufficiency and respond in humility to this undeserved gift we have each received, so that we can follow the advice of the apostle Paul: "Since we have these promises, beloved, let us cleanse ourselves from every defilement of body and spirit, and make holiness perfect in the fear of God" (2 Cor 7:1).

[3] Cf. *CCC*, no. 847, 2001; Second Vatican Council, *Lumen Gentium*, no. 15.

6

We Bought the Cow

For where your treasure is, there will your heart be also.

—Matthew 6:21

One afternoon, after months
of consideration and conster-
nation, and then weeks of
waiting, we finally drove to
an out-of-the-way Mennonite
community to pick up Kristina
and her weaned calf. Kristina
was a two-year-old Jersey, and
the calf was her first (we named
him T-bone so the entire family would accept from the start that he
was destined to be more than a cute pet).

It is safe to say that everyone else in our lives thought we were
fools—that *I* was a fool—for buying a dairy cow. None of this made
any difference, though, once my two older sons had told me, sep-
arately, after several weeks of milking Kristina, "Thanks, Dad, for
getting us the cow," and our four-year-old Richard couldn't stop
petting her. I guess you might say I traded having a membership at
the local golf course for a petting zoo. (In the picture above, Kristina's stall is being used for the annual live nativity, which seems to
have bewildered her.)

My sons Jon Marc and Peter were naturals at milking, whereas
I needed practice. My hands are just too big and clumsy. It wasn't
long, though, before we had fallen into a routine, the two of them
milking together in the evening, one on each side, while I took the

morning shift. Richard was there at both shifts, either petting Kristina or trying to ride the sheep. All together we were harvesting nearly four gallons a day for a family of five! Eventually, we used the excess in cheese making and in feeding a young pig.

At first, Marilyn was reticent about getting involved. I had been convinced that she had given her complete support to this purchase, but on the night before the pickup, she let me know in spades her second thoughts. She insisted I was bringing us into ruin by buying this cow, and she certainly was not going to help milk! In this, she sounded a lot like her mother, who has nothing but bad to say about cows and milking. To this day, Grandma Crown breaks into a panic, her eyes glazing over, when she remembers her daily routine as a young girl milking fourteen cows every morning before school and then again every evening (so she claims).

Marilyn and her relatives might have been right: there's no fool like an old fool, and I'm getting older all the time! It did generally take a little over an hour to milk and feed the cow and then take care of the sheep—a whole lot longer than opening the refrigerator and pulling out a carton of store-bought 2 percent. In time, however, we all came to agree that this was a good thing for our family. Marilyn not only came around to love Kristina and her delicious milk, but she missed Kristina, as we all did, after she died, and she was equally glad when we eventually replaced this void in our lives with another Jersey named Anastasia.

I believe there is an intangible spiritual grace one receives through the hands-on experience of doing things for oneself. It's more than the mere slowness of it, or the labor intensity. I believe we receive grace through physical intimacy with God's creation (more on this to come), which is a reflection of the hypostatic union of Christ's Incarnation. In Catholic jargon, these physical channels of grace are akin to sacramentals, little brothers of the more substantive sacraments. The key to this lies in the idea that what we receive and the quality of what we receive is shaped by what we become intimate with: "For where your treasure is, there will your heart be also" (Mt 6:21).

I first sensed this when I cut by hand the wood to build our "chicken condominium", as Marilyn calls it. It took me several times as long to complete it without the aid of electricity, and it did bless me with a very sore back.

I experienced it again later when I used an old brace-and-bit to drill large holes in fence posts far from a power source, instead of using an expensive battery-driven power drill. This made my back and sternum even sorer, but the silence was precious: when I had finished, I stood up, stretched, turned around, and found our small flock of sheep gathered silently around, their heads titled at the same angle, staring, fascinated.

Or when we developed our freshwater spring and watched the clear, clean spring water flow naturally into our animal troughs without electricity or pumps. Or when my sons and I tore down a hundred-year-old shed and used the locally hewn wooden planks to build partitions and gates in our hundred-year-old barn—rather than buying it all from the local lumberyard or paying someone else to build it. Or when I planted an acre of winter wheat by walking over the freshly plowed field, broadcasting the seed, and then burying it by dragging a handmade harrow behind our tractor. And I sense this every time my sons and I hold in our hands the jars of warm filtered milk we have drawn by hand from the warm udders of our own family cow.

Compare a glass of milk bought from the store with one from our own cow. Where is the intimacy? Where is the channel of grace? That glass of store-bought milk was purchased with money from my wallet or with a check or a credit card. Cash in my wallet or my pocket is closer in intimacy than a check, which draws from a cistern of deposited earnings, or a credit card, which delays payment even further, with the additional step of being paid later with a check. But even the cash that comes from the small assortment of legal tender in my wallet originated from a variety of sources, including my salary, speaking stipends, royalties, birthday gifts from parents, and refunds from returned merchandise or overpaid bills. By the time I spend the cash, I have no way of determining which act or effort it came from. And besides, the money has no obvious connection to the specific work I did anyway; it was merely my reward for services rendered. My intimacy was with the work I did as a writer, speaker, or director.

These avenues of vocation, of course, are totally valid sources of grace, and in these acts of faithfulness I am to seek my holiness. But in that glass of store-bought milk on the table, the intimacy is so far disconnected that it has become merely a means of sustenance. I hope someone else at the source of its production received the grace it could have given. But more likely, in our day, this milk comes from mechanically milked cows in an assembly line of hundreds of cows, by laborers whose mental focus is on what they did the night before or what they hope to do as soon as their workday is over.

In milking our own cow, we experience many forms of direct intimacy: with the barn my sons and I remodeled; with the hay we helped bale and stack in the barn; with the assortment of animals in the barn all baying, baaing, and mooing at us as we enter; with the tenderness of their glances as they await their morning sustenance; and then with the physicality of the cow as I lead her to her milking station, feed her a bountiful trough of grain, wash her teats, and then massage the milk out by hand into a bucket I have sterilized. When done, I thank Kristina with loving rubs and words and lead her back into her stall. I feed her, her calf, T-bone, and our nine sheep. Then in the kitchen, after my long walk back up the hill to the house, I strain the milk into clean jars, and there before me is rich, white, wholesome milk. After grinding a handful of coffee beans, I make a fresh cup of coffee. While this is brewing, I use a small ladle to remove some fresh cream from the top of last night's milk and have a warm cup of coffee with this cream my boys and I drew from our own cow. (This fresh raw milk, by the way, is fully "pasteurized" and "homogenized", because our cow is fed on "pasture" and is milked only by "genus homo sapiens".)

It isn't pride, though I'm sure some is in there. And it isn't just a sense of satisfaction for doing it ourselves rather than merely paying someone else to do it for us. There is something deeper, which I truly believe is a grace—but only a grace communicated in the process of our intimacy with all these things, creatures, and acts. The key to this is that we do it with hearts that recognize and thank God for all these gifts of His mercy and love. By His grace, our hearts have been opened to recognize that all these things are His gifts to us. By our willing response to His grace, we thank Him for our home, our land, our animals, our health, our time, our growing patience, and more recently, the strength and coordination of our fingers. Through all this we receive more grace—and the intimacy of His divine life.

I guess the point here is that God desires to communicate His grace in a myriad of ways, and not just through the seven sacraments—though these are the normal and certain means of grace. What we each need to do is discern the additional physical channels God has provided to communicate His grace to our families. For most people, milking a cow, planting a field, remodeling a barn, collecting eggs, writing a book, giving a speech, hosting a television program, or merely skimming off cream for the morning coffee are all acts of intimacy they cannot do for lack of time, health, opportunities, or resources. For some, as was the case with my father, just getting out of bed, walking to the kitchen table, and breathing life-sustaining oxygen from a cylinder take all the effort and concentration they can muster. But the key is recognizing that whatever God has specifically given us to do for this day can be a channel through which He desires to give us grace—so that we might grow closer to Him and more in His likeness. What makes this possible are tender hearts of gratitude, which express with and in each act, "Thank You, Lord, for all the gifts You've given us."

As I thought about this later in the day on which the sheep watched me drill those holes, it became more apparent that there is something unique about those intimate, grace-filled actions that connect more directly with our basic needs than those that don't. Regardless, as Saint Paul said long ago, "Whatever your task, work heartily, as serving the Lord and not men, knowing that from the Lord you will receive the inheritance as your reward; you are serving the Lord Christ" (Col 3:23–24) and, "[W]hether you eat or drink, or whatever you do, do all to the glory of God" (1 Cor 10:31).

But Why Milk?

Some still may question why anyone would waste time milking a cow each and every morning and evening, seven days a week, twelve months a year, when he could just as easily go down to the local convenience store and buy all the milk, butter, cheese, and yogurt he could possibly need. Good question. I suppose I have asked myself

that question many times, especially when it's five degrees below zero and I'm out at six A.M., trying to locate our Jersey's teats with frozen fingers, through the fog of my breath.

I could formulate an idealistic and philosophical answer, but the question is really more simply answered by recognizing that, over the past two hundred years especially, with the advent of every modern convenience, choices had to be made as to whether doing something the old way was better, more satisfying, or more time consuming, et cetera, than doing something the new way. One doesn't need to look very far, however, to see that, as beneficial and necessary as modern conveniences might seem, something is always potentially lost in the move toward saving time, energy, and effort.

It used to be that to enjoy music in the home or in the community, people needed to take music lessons. Millions of people could play the piano, or the accordion, the violin, the flute, the harmonica, the guitar, and even the tuba. Almost every community had a band or an orchestra. Sunday afternoons were spent playing in or listening to the local band, or sitting around the fire playing in the family ensemble, or sitting at the keyboard, enjoying Bach, Chopin, or Beethoven. But with the advent of radio, movies, television, records, tapes, CDs, videos, MP3s, iTunes, et cetera, the number of people who play their own music has drastically dwindled. Why go to all the effort to learn how to play it ourselves when it is cheaper, less time consuming, and maybe even more relaxing just to sit back with headphones and listen to our favorite downloaded MP3?

Why learn to carve wood when anything can be bought at the local China-outlet department store?

Why paint with oils and brush, or draw with straightedge and pencil, when we can do it all with computer-aided graphics?

Why walk when we can ride—or even fly?

Why read when we can listen or view or even take part virtually through a computer?

Why sew, darn, mend, or knit when everything we could possibly need to wear can be bought for a pittance around the corner?

Most of what we know about the lives of people in the past has come from their diaries, but who keeps diaries anymore when every "important" event of our lives is shared with the world instantaneously on social media?

The list goes on and on. I guess the answers to these questions lie in how we choose to use and focus our time, energies, and efforts. I do not think, nor am I advocating, that everyone ought to return to milking their own family cow, woodcarving, playing piano, filling a journal with illegible scribbles, or walking to work. I am asserting, though, what so many others have tried to tell us: that as a society we have lost something essential when we so easily justify moving on to quicker, easier, and less *self*-energy-consuming activities.

Over the last three days, I milked the cow six times, which also involved feeding and watering the animals; I helped birth a baby goat; and I made cheddar cheese, butter, buttermilk pancakes, cottage cheese, and ricotta cheese. I also enjoyed several brisk and crisp morning walks in our woods out to the barn; I spoke often to our six sheep, our Jersey cow and calf, our two cats, our two dogs, our mama and kid goats, and our two chickens; and while sitting there milking, I had lots of time to pray, ponder, and grow in the virtue of patience.

I've come to see that the main thing we have lost as a society and as individuals, in unapologetically accepting the modernist belief in progress and all its effects, is our ability to slow down, to wait on the Lord, and to listen quietly.

Update

Well, to be honest, I wrote the above thirteen years ago, and frankly, my muscles ache just to think of what I was able to do back then! That wonderful Jersey cow, named Kristina, has long since passed on to that big pasture in the sky, and our new Jersey, Anastasia, is dried

up until her next calving. Since those sheep, our pastures have seen
an assortment of other critters, and now we're down to a half dozen
Angus cattle. We're back up to fifteen chickens, though, giving us a
dozen or more eggs a day, and who knows how many cats and dogs
we have at any given moment.

The main thing, however, is how little I myself have listened to
my own words these past thirteen years. Just think about how far
and fast, in just this past decade, our world has descended down the
modernist progressive path; how, as a culture, we are even less able
to slow down, wait on the Lord, and listen quietly; how, in our culture, the freed-up time, talents, and energy we have reaped from our
unexamined addiction to every new technology have instead been
redirected into such meaningless, time-consuming activities and too
often into unanticipated, often immoral choices and lifestyles. And
the entanglements we have brought upon ourselves and our families
are almost impossible to break. Just think about how much money
most of us spend every month on entertainment and communication
services that twenty-five years ago we never even imagined having,
let alone financing. Of course, for most of us, the impact of these
expenditures is assuaged because we've set them up as automatic
withdrawals—we don't even have to expend time, energy, and effort
in paying for our entanglements!

There is something particularly significant in all of this: a year ago,
after a ten-year hiatus, our family began milking again. We purchased
Anastasia, and I quickly discovered how, even after a few weeks'
practice, I could not physically milk a cow as I used to—not just
because of the beginning signs of arthritis, but because my muscles
had lost their edge.

Ever try to use any of the everyday tools of yesteryear? Ever try
to cut down a tree with a two-man crosscut saw rather than a chain-
saw? Ever try to dig a ditch with a shovel rather than a tractor and
backhoe? Ever try to go back to handwriting a diary after using
only a computer for ten-plus years? It's nearly impossible to go back
because the necessary muscles have either atrophied or never developed. I believe this is also true for the spiritual, emotional, and mental
muscles of our culture. Generally, when we try to simplify our lives,
we give up quickly because it requires far more effort than we're
willing or able to give.

Consider this provocative quote:

A brute animal cannot form an idea of a table because the idea is spiritual whereas an animal is material and nothing else. Therefore, as often as a man makes a table, a chair, a barn, or anything else, he is acting in a way that proclaims him to be more than a brute animal. He is exercising that faculty which, because it distinguishes him from a beast, is more important than his body. As a maker of things, man functions spiritually and materially. Consequently, for the ordinary man to use things continually that have been made by a machine, or to work mechanically at a task that requires no exercise of his spiritual faculty, is to deaden that faculty and to make him less a man in the very thing which proclaims him to be a man and not a beast. This point looms large in a consideration of modern industrialism.[1]

This statement was written in 1940 in a book entitled *Rural Roads to Security*, warning about the encroaching effects of industrialism. I wonder what the author would say if he could visit us today, seventy-five years later? Does this at least partially explain why the new "moralities" of our culture are more indicative of "brute animals"?

So what's the answer? Well, that's personal, of course, and given my previous thirteen-year record, I'm hardly the one to give advice. But I think at least one answer can be found somewhere in our efforts to break free so that we can once again—or maybe for the first time in our lives—slow down, wait on the Lord, and listen to Him quietly: "But when you pray, go into your room and shut the door and pray to your Father who is in secret; and your Father who sees in secret will reward you" (Mt 6:6).

Are there ways in which you could become closer to the means of grace that God has provided through His creation, especially through His Church? Merely saying "Thank You, Lord" and acknowledging Him in even the most menial task can turn that task into a powerful channel of grace and peace (see Phil 4:6–7). Do you have a place in your life where you can "shut the door" and retreat from the entanglements and enticements of modern technology, or are you so entangled that you can't even imagine life without them?

[1] L. Ligutti and J. C. Rawe, *Rural Roads to Security: America's Third Struggle for Freedom* (Milwaukee: Bruce, 1940), 54.

The apostle John ended his first letter very abruptly! Without any semblance of a closing, he wrote simply, "Little children, keep yourselves from idols" (5:21). Maybe this was because there was nothing more significant he could have said: anything in our lives that distracts us from God—from seeing His fingerprints and creative love in the world around us—can become an idol. The enticing modern technologies that have made our modern world run so smoothly and efficiently and have filled our lives with leisure and made our muscles and minds too flabby for us to exert ourselves to do anything creative or challenging—have these entanglements become our new idols? Lord, help us to free ourselves from the things in which we have already become impotently entangled and to keep ourselves from them, so that we can prevent our children and grandchildren from becoming as entangled as we.

7

Straight Paths

*Therefore lift your drooping hands and strengthen your
weak knees, and make straight paths for your feet, so that
what is lame may not be put out of joint but rather be
healed. Strive for peace with all men, and for the holiness
without which no one will see the Lord.*

—Hebrews 12:12–14

Last night, I was out mowing a field. As I precariously drove my tractor up a slope along a fence line, I remembered how that fence line had looked fifteen years before, when my family moved from the city onto our country property. Most of our  rolling acreage was overgrown with scrub trees, spicebushes, brambles, and multiflora rose. It was a mess, and most seemed of little value. It was obvious what "leaving it to nature" had produced.

At the time, we had no experience in farming, and with few actively farming neighbors, there weren't many people to ask what we should do. With what we gleaned from conversations and reading, however, we began chipping away at the mess, with hand clippers, axes, chain saws, string trimmers, a tractor, a front loader, and the all-powerful brush hog. We also enrolled the help of a variety of critters: cattle, sheep, a horse, chickens, and pigs. Every year, with what time and energy we could muster, we made improvements, rebuilding fence rows, toppling unwanted or dead trees, uprooting bramble bushes, developing springs, and improving the quality of the pastures through mowing and grazing.

It is important to admit that we weren't always sure, or agreed, about the direction in which we were going with our "farm". To this day, I'm hesitant to use this term, for I've grown to have nothing but awesome respect for the diligence and intelligence of our American farmers—especially those who have gone before us, doing so much more with so much less. Often, at that time, all I knew was that something right before me needed to be done: if we didn't do it right away, it might never get done, and it would only grow worse.

Then last night, as I drove my tractor and mower up the now-smooth slope and saw extending before me a beautiful expansive field of timothy, clover, and other nutritious grasses and legumes, I remembered what it was like before and how, without revealing the full blueprints, God has guided us over the years, one step at a time.

Growing in holiness is a lot like the progress on our land. Jesus said that the central commandments for His followers were to love God and to love one another. The rest of the New Testament is essentially about how to live this out. As the author of Hebrews put it so succinctly: "Strive for peace with all men, and for *the holiness without which no one will see the Lord*" (Heb 12:14, emphasis mine).

Holiness is how we live out our loving of God with heart, mind, soul, and strength, and if we cannot "see the Lord" without this holiness, what must we do to make sure we are becoming holy?

There are, of course, far, far wiser spiritual writers than I who have addressed this, in books and in other media. Of course, all that we have in the Church is directed toward this end, especially the sacraments, our liturgical worship and devotions, and works of mercy.

Often holiness has been described as a process of growing to be like Christ, one small step after another, much like the adage about how to eat an elephant: one bite at a time. In Jesus' parable of the talents, for example, He emphasized the necessity of being faithful in a little so that one [or we] may be trusted with more (Mt 25:14–30). In His Sermon on the Mount, He also alluded to this process: "[S]eek first his kingdom and his righteousness, and all these things shall be yours as well. Therefore do not be anxious about tomorrow, for tomorrow will be anxious for itself. Let the day's own trouble be sufficient for the day" (Mt 6:33–34). In other words, our present moment is our first responsibility; the long-term effect of our present efforts is beyond our present view. We can move forward only in trust, knowing that our present obedience, or disobedience, will have a cumulative and eternal result.

Guiding my tractor up, over, and around a hilltop, I remembered when I had reseeded that pasture several years before. This incident made me think of my favorite passage from Proverbs:

> Trust in the LORD with all your heart,
>   and do not rely on your own insight.
> In all your ways acknowledge him,
>   and he will *make straight your paths*.
>   (3:5–6, emphasis mine)

I had gone out to overseed our east pasture with clover the old-fashioned way, with a hand-cranked spreader. As I began, the question arose as to how I was going to keep my "paths straight" enough to spread the seeds evenly. I first learned what I thought was an adequate answer long ago as a young boy when my father lovingly placed my hands on the lawn mower. After watching me make a few wavy, haphazard rows, he set down his iced tea, ran out, and said, "Son, don't focus downward at the mower at your feet; look straight ahead to the end of the row. Avoid glancing down any more than necessary; just focus ahead on your destination, and trust."

At first, I found this awkward—I was sure I would leave lines of uncut grass—but eventually I got brave enough to do an entire row without looking down, and lo and behold, the path was straight with no missed grass. As I grew in courage, my anxieties waned, and soon I could cut the entire yard with nary a downward glance of doubt.

This experience grew into a regular preaching image for the fifteen years that I served as a youth and pastoral minister, with obvious allusions: "We need to keep our eyes firmly fixed on Jesus, laying 'aside every weight [distraction], and sin which clings so closely, and let us run with perseverance the race that is set before us, looking to Jesus the pioneer and perfecter of our faith' (Heb 12:1–2). We must not be like Peter, who took his eye off Jesus and sank (Mt 14:28–31); we need to ignore the distractions and fears of life and focus directly on Him and trust!"

This was a good analogy, as was my father's advice, as far as it went. Over time, though, I discovered its flaws. You see, I grew up in northwestern Ohio, where our half-acre backyard was as flat as a bowling alley. Focusing straight ahead was just that—straight ahead. Since then I've never had a yard that wasn't undulated, and now there isn't a flat spot on our twenty-five acres of Appalachian foothills. As I glanced ahead across the rolling field toward my destination, I saw trees and thorn bushes I would have to maneuver around and hundreds of cow pies and horse piles I would have to avoid carefully. Plus, due to spring rains, I would mostly be trudging through ankle-deep mud.

Life is much like this. God's promise, as expressed in the aforementioned verses from Proverbs, to "make straight [our] paths" does not necessarily mean that we will be able to plot a clearly discernible path or that our life in Jesus—past, present, and future—will all make sense. "Now I see what He was doing and why He led me to do that!" This certainly is sometimes true, but I have come to see that the straightness of what God does to our paths, by grace, is an aspect not so much of direction, but of holiness. Proverbs speaks here of the mysterious partnership we have with God in our salvation: His sovereign will and our freedom of will to choose. We are called to listen to Him and, in response, to turn from ourselves in His direction willingly and freely. In the process, we are also called to realize that somehow in the mystery of His mercy, He was the One who imbued our actions with grace. We are fully responsible for trusting in Him with our whole hearts, yet it is He who makes us straight, adjusting not just our course as we "press on toward the goal for the prize of the upward call of God in Christ Jesus" (Phil 3:14) but also our very selves, right now, wherever we are in life, making us straight and upright, after His own posture of holiness.

In the mystery of His loving plan for each of us, God strives through grace to make us holy in each of the many undulations in our desire to follow His calling. Making straight our paths does not mean that He rids our lives of suffering, sadness, frustration, discouragement, radical changes in course, or even failure. It is, in fact, in the midst of these things—and why He allows them to happen—that we are most called to trust fully in Him, not to rely on our own insight, to acknowledge Him in everything, and to proceed ahead, believing that He is making our lives straight—in other words, holy.

All of this reminds me of an even more poignant agrarian analogy used by Christ, one that I never fully appreciated until I ventured to farm this land: "Jesus said to him, 'No one who puts his hand to the plow and looks back is fit for the kingdom of God'" (Lk 9:62). Anyone who mows a yard or plows a field while looking backward quickly learns the truth of this axiom. Recently, after an eight-inch snowfall had covered all the flaws of our land with a smooth, pristine white blanket, I allowed my youngest son, Richard, to have his first try at using the tractor and blade to clear our long, winding driveway. For his first attempt, he did amazingly well—much better than my first attempt! But as he passed the house, with joyful pride, he began looking back to see whether his mother was watching. After several seconds of this, he not only had left the curved and narrow edge of the driveway but had started a new "driveway" down over the embankment.

Lots of things can distract us from making straight our paths. Sometimes it's the "suffering, sadness, frustration, discouragement, radical changes in course, or even failure" that remain or even seem to increase after we've chosen to put our hands to the plow of following and serving Christ. We think back to less stressful times, or we look enviously at the lives of others. Sometimes the hardest hurdle for me to get over, when I'm bundling up in the early morning to go out into single-digit weather to make the long hike to the barn to take care of our livestock, is to refrain from thinking of my friends who have *not* chosen this rural life—who are at that moment relaxing cozily with their feet up, in their suburban homes, sipping cappuccinos, watching the morning news, reading their Bibles, or praying, with no sense of "guilt" that there is anything else they need to do.

Maybe we are most distracted, though, by our vanity: wondering whether anyone is watching, admiring, and praising our progress and accomplishments. The more we become caught up in this, the more the plow swerves, and the less fit we become for the kingdom of God.

No one has ever said it better than John the Baptist: "He must increase, but I must decrease" (Jn 3:30).

As I sat back that evening long ago, after overseeding five muddy acres, sore and soggy from working for six hours in abnormally hot seventy-degree March weather, I felt a noble sense of accomplishment.

I was confident that this was exactly what God had called me to do in a timely manner in those last weeks of winter.

But then, after two days of continuous drenching rain, and with our county under a flood warning, I wondered whether any of the clover seed remained or whether we'd end up with thick clover patches along the drainage ditches.

Had it all been a waste? I suppose in a material sense some might consider it a waste, but ultimately what is important is the condition and attitude of my heart: *then* as I was doing it, *now* as I look back, and *tomorrow* as I once again seek to live out my favorite passage from Proverbs.

As I enter into my "twilight years", I fully recognize that what my family and I are able to do now on this land, we could not do except for what we have previously done year after year—and all, of course, because of the gracious gifts from God of this property and resources; of our children, family, and friends; of time; and of our health.

I believe more and more that what is most important is not anything about our past, or about where we might be or what we might have in the future, but about how we are being faithful right now, in the present moment, with what we have and what we have been given.

The past is gone. The only element of the past that can become a present necessity is an offense for which we need to make amends or seek forgiveness. This must be fixed if it has been neglected, for otherwise, like an unkept field, it will only grow into an unsurpassable wall of briars.

The future, on the other hand, is but an unfathomable concoction of our efforts and the grace of God. Since we have no way of knowing for certain our future, we can only focus every effort on being humbly obedient in the present moment, knowing that God will work "for good with those who love him, who are called according to his purpose" (Rom 8:28). Or again, as summarized in that proverb: "Trust in the LORD with all your heart, and do not rely on your own insight. In all your ways acknowledge him, and he will make straight your paths" (Prov 3:5–6).

As I was finishing up the mowing last night, I turned my tractor around a large walnut tree and was stopped abruptly by a strange, unexpected sight. Here, passing slowing across the open field, was a mama possum carrying her brood of babies. None of them showed any fear. In fact, the baby possums, bouncing along bright-eyed to the world, trusting completely in the patient gait of their mother, seemed calmly thrilled by the sight of me and my large tractor. "Wow! Look at that! Wonder what it is!"

Have we lost the trusting thrill of our present moment? Regardless of our present financial situation, we too can know that the patient gait of our Creator and Father has nothing but good in store for those of us who thankfully seek, one step at a time, to make straight our paths and grow in His likeness. "Not that I complain of want; for I have learned, in whatever state I am, to be content" (Phil 4:11).

Oh, and by the mercy of God, those clover seeds I planted years ago did take root everywhere I planted them.

8

Sometimes Why Is Not Why

A man's mind plans his way,
but the LORD directs his steps.

—Proverbs 16:9

Admittedly, my interest in devoting too much of my time and energy to this "farm" has waxed and waned. I fully realize that I'm not a natural farmer, and not having grown up on a farm or around farmers is a nearly insurmountable weakness. The FFA kids whom I, as

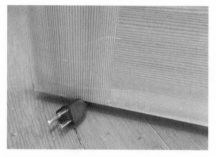

a city dweller, used to lampoon while growing up had more usable knowledge about farming in their little fingers than I will ever gain in this short life. *Mea culpa!* Whenever I pray for assistance with some farm task, the consistent message I receive from the communion of saints is, "Don't give up your day job."

Besides, there is no place more fertile for the infestation of Murphy's Law than the farm! Certainly we all have experienced the occasional demoralizing taunts of Murphy's Law: carry an armload of shirts, and a hanger grabs a doorknob; carry an armload of groceries in your left arm, and your car keys are in your left pants pocket; move the vacuum around the house, and the plug catches under a door. The list goes on endlessly.

Well, on the farm, the list increases exponentially, at least for me, in direct proportion to the number of ambitious chores I plan: every big task requires at least three trips to Tractor Supply or Lowes; if I need a Phillips screwdriver, I can find only flatheads (and vice versa); every plug on every piece of equipment always catches on something along the way; I'm all set to cut a cord of wood, and the gas can is empty; and generally I always need a third hand to get anything done when I'm alone on the back acres.

For a while, I wondered whether these demoralizing interruptions were demonic (Is this happening only to me!), or if they were angelic messengers from God trying to tell me that I had misheard God's call (not "farming" but "framing": He intended for me to work in a photo shop!).

In time, though, I think I've come to understand Murphy's Law: it's an active strategy of God's desire to purge us of attitudes that prevent us from being fruitful (see Jn 15:2). As the author of Hebrews wrote, "The Lord disciplines him whom he loves, and chastises every son whom he receives" (12:6).

Now, whenever I need a hammer out in the barn and realize that they're all up at the house, three hundred yards away, or I bump my six-foot-four-inch-high head for the thousandth time on the five-foot-ten rafters in our hundred-year-old sheep barn, or I can't read the minute ingredients on a feedbag because I forgot to wear my bifocals, or I get my tractor immovably bound up on a hidden stump in the weeds, I just smile and know that this is all a sign that God loves me and only wants me to grow in humility.

All this is to say that there have been many "signs" calling into question whether I should devote so much of my time, talents, energy, and resources to developing this land into a farm.

Is Our Son Called to Be a Farmer?

As it became more and more obvious that our youngest son, Richard, was not a "traditional learner" (at least not in the eyes of our modern educational system) and probably not college bound, the question arose whether we could interest him in learning to farm. Could he maybe develop and farm a portion of our land? At sixteen, he seemed interested, so together he and I decided to prepare our acreage to graze cattle rotationally. We spent several months mowing and cleaning up about ten acres and then used temporary electric fencing to divide the acres into paddocks, ensuring that each paddock had access to water. Then, with great excitement, we bought six Angus feeder calves. All of this to explore whether this might be the calling of our youngest son.

Together we learned what needed to be done daily to care for and move the cattle from one paddock to the next. We learned that we had become, not cattle farmers, but grass farmers: we were using the cattle to mow our fields. As the first winter approached, when other small farmers were taking their well-fed feeder calves to market, we decided together to keep ours over the winter, as the start of our grass-fed herd. This required stocking the barn with hay. In the meantime, we had added to our herd our Jersey cow Anastasia, and so we were back into daily milking. All of this to explore whether this might be the calling of our youngest son.

During the winter, the rotational schedule ceased, but in the spring, the rotations returned. In time, we were gifted with three calves. Also, in the spring, we got back into poultry farming and added sixteen chickens to our menagerie, blessing us with range-fed eggs. Then, after distributing a load of our personally cultured cow manure, we planted an eighty-by-twenty-foot garden, which flourished! All of this to explore whether this might be the calling of our youngest son.

Then something became progressively clear over the winter and the spring: farming is not, as far as we could tell, Richard's calling. The onset of Murphy's Law in his life, whenever he comes out to help me with farm chores, is far more serious than mere spiritual discipline: it is downright dangerous, even life threatening. As they say, the farm is the most dangerous place in America for children (at least it used to be). It also became obvious that Richard was hungrier for social interaction and a vocation out with people than for the solitary, self-contented life of modern small farming.

In time, the cattle became my primary chore, and Marilyn and I shared responsibilities for the milking, the chickens, and the garden.

Richard would help, if push came to shove, but it was not where his heart was, nor, frankly, his gifts. (UPDATE: I must note with joy that Richard is a great help to his Aunt Holly harvesting apples and making homemade cider.)

Man's Plans Are Not God's Plans

The writer of Proverbs once said, "There are many plans in a man's heart, nevertheless the LORD's counsel—that will stand" (19:21, NKJV). As I write, we are in the middle of the snowiest January on record. My daily morning task is to bundle up and walk the three hundred yards across the valley, through six-inch-deep snow, to the barn to care for our cattle. An incident happened recently that is worth sharing.

Last Friday, temperatures overnight had dropped to single digits, with an additional snowfall of three inches. I trudged out to the barn, barely awake from my morning coffee. My mind was farther ahead of me, reviewing a long list of plans and tasks I felt were necessary to complete before the weekend. I loaded a bucket of grain mix to feed our five remaining cattle. Since a cow's conscience has no file folder for sharing, I generally wait until all five have taken their places beside the communal trough before distributing the feed.

This particular morning only four arrived—missing was the runt, a nine-month-old pitch-black Angus heifer calf. She looks more like a large dog than a beef cow. I called and called (i.e., mooed), but there was no response. Eventually, I noticed some movement about a hundred feet up the frozen hill, near a pile of fallen branches. I struggled up the steep, snow-covered slope, careful not to slip or trip over the myriad of frozen cow divots in our mostly clay soil. As I approached, I saw the young calf on her side, caught in the branches. My heart began beating furiously. Sometime during the night, the poor calf had lain down or fallen into the brush pile with her legs lying uphill, making it impossible for her to right herself. By the time I found her, she had bloodied herself in trying to escape and had become frozen to the ground.

I cleared away the branches and snow. I tried to help her up, but her front knee was frozen solid in ice. I cautiously retraced my steps back to the barn and returned with a heavy iron spud bar. With this, I carefully chipped her leg free, but still she could not stand. She was limp from the cold and lack of food. I tried to move her, but in the ice and snow, I could get no leverage. I tried to drag her down the slope, but the frozen cow divots acted like razor-sharp speed bumps. I returned to the barn to get my tractor so that I could move her using the front loader, but the tractor motor was frozen. I plugged in the engine heater, but this solution would take hours, so I returned to the calf with a blanket, some grain, and water. She devoured the feed but refused the water. I used all the energy I could muster to hoist her onto a piece of cardboard to insulate her from the frozen ground.

Through the kitchen window Marilyn eventually noticed me lying spread-eagled in the snow on the far hillside. She and Richard rushed out, bundled against the frigid cold, with more blankets and a windbreak—and my cell phone, which, against house rules, I had forgotten! I called the only large-animal veterinarian in the region. Already busy delivering several calves at other frozen farms, he promised to come when he could.

For several hours we nursed the calf out on the blowing hillside, until the vet finally arrived. Together we trudged up the hill to the calf, carrying water and equipment, to pump her full of a Gatorade-like electrolyte solution. Other than a few shots of medications, there was little more the vet could do. He wasn't hopeful or particularly sympathetic, noting that a true "cattleman" would hardly concern himself over the death of such an obviously undersized calf.

Once the tractor had finally started, Richard and I loaded her carefully into the front loader and transported her to an isolated stall in the barn. There we nested her in straw and made the stall windproof and snow proof, nursing her through the rest of the afternoon and evening. Needless to say, I accomplished nothing on my long list of "necessary" plans and tasks.

Saturday brought more snow and temperatures in the teens, and along with other farm and home chores, we continued to nurse the struggling calf. She would gobble food but refused water. She would

try to stand but could do little
more than push herself around
in the straw. I tried to lift and
help her, but her front legs
hung limp. Interestingly, before
this incident, she had refused to
let us get close to her and had
showed natural fear whenever
our dogs wandered close to the

pasture. Now she seemed to welcome my presence, nestling close
whenever I petted her or scratched her cheeks. One time, Bungie,
our large, curly, black dog, followed me cautiously into her stall. The
calf and Bungie touched noses, reminding me of Adam and God
touching fingers in Michelangelo's painting. While I petted the calf,
Bungie licked her.

Nighttime came and passed with little improvement.

Sunday brought more of the same, until late in the evening, when
I trudged out for one last look. On the way over, with no snow fall-
ing and the night clear and crisp, I prayed for some merciful sign from
God that our efforts weren't in vain. If the calf still could not stand on
her own, I would face no other option but to put her down. I wondered whether, with the infinite array of other far more urgent needs
around the globe, I should even presume upon God to ask for help
with such a seemingly insignificant matter. In the beam of a flashlight,
I found the calf resting safely upon her chest. I placed water before
her. She sniffed and looked as if again she would reject it, but to my
surprise, she struggled, first up onto her back legs, then onto her
front knees, and finally, cautiously, wobbling onto all fours. She then
buried her nuzzle into the water and drank two full buckets. Down
again, safe in the soft straw, she looked up at me with her dark cow
eyes, not unlike those of a puppy, with a stare that I'm convinced was
her only way of telling me, "Thanks."

So Now What?

I do not want to give some triumphalist impression that it is a simple
and clear decision to leave the more comfortable and familiar urban
setting for some idyllic peaceful life under the rural stars. I look out

now from our back porch at that barn and consider all the plans we've had for this land, this "farm". As I first penned this chapter, our dearly beloved Jersey cow, Anastasia, was close to giving birth. It was frigid and frozen outside, and I was convinced, in the light of many factors, that we reluctantly would have to find her another home, with a younger family, with more hands to share in the labor and more time to devote to this wonderful work. Then one day at work I got the call from Marilyn that God had blessed us with a beautiful Jersey-Angus bull calf. Without skipping a beat, even with these aching arthritic fingers, I was back in the milking saddle again.

At least for a while.

Anastasia had always had a defective left hip. For milking, she was the perfect designer cow, for she would hold her stiff leg up like a ballerina, giving us easy access. But this also caused her to walk with a limp, and over the past year, it had progressively gotten worse. Our muddy rolling hills didn't make it easy for her either.

Six weeks after giving birth, she slipped in the mud after a torrential spring rain, and we could do nothing to get her to stand again. After a week of diligent tender care and physical therapy, the vet confirmed that we really had only one option. So, with a Ruger 22, I had to do something I had never anticipated when we moved out to this rural land.

Our plans are not always God's plans, but an essential part of continual conversion involves recognizing more and more that His plans are always best.

The great Christian writer C. S. Lewis once said, "The great thing, if one can, is to stop regarding all the unpleasant things as interruptions of one's 'own' or 'real' life. The truth is of course that what one calls the interruptions are precisely one's real life—the life God is sending one day by day; what one calls one's 'real life' is a phantom of one's own imagination."[1]

---

[1] C. S. Lewis to Arthur Greeves, December 20, 1943, in *Yours, Jack: Spiritual Direction from C. S. Lewis* (New York: HarperCollins, 2008), 97–98.

So why did God call us to expend all this time, talent, energy, and *money* on this cattle venture? Just to test whether our son was called to become a farmer? Or maybe to see whether we had it in us to be cattle (grass) farmers? I think it's all akin to those experiences with Murphy's Law. The times when my sons and I were out together working on fences, chasing cattle between paddocks, milking cows, herding sheep, cleaning up fallen trees, splitting wood, stacking hay, losing our boots in knee-deep mud, laughing at the human expressions on the cows' faces or in their moos, shoveling manure into a pile and then transferring it to our garden, repairing the chicken house, building blinds for deer hunting, nursing a rejected lamb back to life in diapers in front of our woodstove, or spending almost an entire weekend nursing back to life a frozen calf who in anyone else's book isn't worth saving—all these experiences in themselves were reason enough; all of this is why.

If I focused on whether I am a profitable cattle farmer or whether our test was successful in making our youngest son a farmer, I might conclude that it was all a failure. But when I think of the experiences we have had together in doing it, and continue to have—a father, a mother, our three sons, and now a daughter-in-law and two grandchildren—I can only smile and know that God loves us.

Sometimes what we think is why is often not why at all.

9

Our Economic Future (and Limits Theory)

*Then they said, "Come, let us build ourselves a city,
and a tower with its top in the heavens, and let us make
a name for ourselves, lest we be scattered abroad upon the
face of the whole earth."*

—Genesis 11:4

As I relax on our back porch, sipping my drink of choice, surveying with glee a freshly mowed lawn and a garden that doesn't yet need weeding, many things pass through these old brain cells of mine. Given the daily news, they all seem to coalesce around the concerns of our present economic culture—more specifically, how my family and I are to live out our lives and our faith in this modern, industrial, progressivist, politically unstable world.

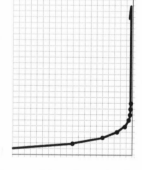

A brain synapse sparked, and I remembered something from a calculus class many, many years ago, something called limits theory. Now, I've certainly forgotten far more than I ever learned, but I remember a graph associated with an old conundrum called Zeno's dichotomy paradox. If you are standing five feet from a wall and start walking toward it, with each step equal to half the remaining distance to the wall, how many steps and how long will it take you to reach the wall? The answer in both cases is infinite; in other words, you'll never reach the wall. You'll get increasingly closer, but with each step you will reach only half the distance between you and the wall.

There are several ways to visualize this conundrum, but one way is with the graph above. Each dot and the vertical increase of one unit represent each step halfway horizontally toward the wall. (Now, all you mathematicians and economists out there, take a breather—I'm doing the best I can.)

What amazes me is how this graph seems to depict everything in our present modern human condition. Take, for example, the *history of communications*. If the horizontal axis of this graph represents time, then each dot represents the great advancements in communication throughout the history of mankind. Mankind went for centuries with only verbal or hand communications and scratching out symbols on rocks. Long-distance communication required either yelling more loudly and waving more emphatically, or sending out messengers ("apostles"), or passing around dried-mud cuneiform tablets. Then someone invented papyrus and paper and chalk and ink and quills and binding, but still, for centuries distant communication was limited to screaming, messengers, and hand copying.

Then movable type came along, and printing, and mass publishing, and then fountain pens, typewriters, telegraph, telephones, loudspeakers, radio, television, computers, cell phones, Internet, e-mail, texting, smartphones, social networking, et cetera, et cetera, et cetera, and you get my drift. Again, note the acceleration of these advancements, or should I say, changes, in how we communicate. Now, with every single day bringing some new communications advancement and product, it hardly pays to buy anything, because by tomorrow it will be obsolete. We have no way of identifying or predicting the trajectory or goal of this progress in communications. We are living on the vertical accelerating slope of a communications revolution that has no foreseeable destination.

Take, for another example, the *history of travel*. For many centuries, men traveled on foot; then came the use of critters, then the wheel, then carriages, chariots, and wagons. These improvements carried men for centuries, until the industrial age brought the bicycle, the steamship, the train, and the automobile, and then the airplane and space travel and the Segway Personal Transporter and on and on.

What is significant, illustrated by the graph, is that the acceleration of these advancements has reached such breakneck speed that we really have no way of projecting where travel will be in fifty, twenty-five, five years, or even one year from now. Nor can we identify the trajectory or goal of this progress in transportation. We are living on the vertical accelerating slope of a travel revolution that has no foreseeable destination.

This same historical accelerating phenomenon is true of nearly every aspect of our lives: trade, information, markets, clothing styles, goods and services, medical care and insurance, and particularly *change* itself. There was a time when people lived their entire lives with little changes in any of these things: from the time they were born until they died, they barely saw changes in clothing, communication, travel, cuisine, or even politics.

For us who live on the vertical slope of change in everything, the anxiety of trying to live in this accelerating, goalless culture of presumed progress is also accelerating, as illustrated by the man in the graph on the right. This explains why this graph also depicts the acceleration of crime and drugs, divorce and broken lives, even the previously unimagined acceptance of immoral lifestyles, as well as the increase in suicides and interest in euthanasia.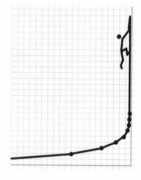

Significantly, the graph also depicts the rise in our national, global, and personal debt and, interestingly, the historic rise in persecution and martyrdoms of those who try to stand for what has always been known as right, true, and beautiful. It even depicts the increasing challenges to our religious freedom in this "land of the free and home of the brave".

This entire scenario reminds me of a quote about industrialism:

> The tempo of the industrial life is fast, but that is not the worst of it; it is accelerating. The ideal is not merely some set form of industrialism, with so many stable industries, but industrial progress, or an incessant extension of industrialization. It never proposes a specific goal; it initiates the infinite series. We have not merely capitalized certain industries; we have capitalized the laboratories and inventors, and undertaken to employ all the labor-saving devices that come out of them. But a fresh labor-saving device introduced into an industry does not emancipate the laborers in that industry so much as it evicts them.

Of course no single labor-saving process is fatal; it brings on a period of unemployed labor and unemployed capital, but soon a new industry is devised which will put them both to work again, and a new commodity is thrown upon the market.

All might yet be well, and stability and comfort might again obtain, but for this: partly because of industrial ambitions and partly because the repressed creative impulse must break out somewhere, there will be a stream of further labor-saving devices in all industries, and the cycle will have to be repeated over and over. The result is an increasing disadjustment and instability.[1]

The above quote comes from the introduction, "A Statement of Principles", to the book *I'll Take My Stand: The South and the Agrarian Tradition*, by Twelve Southerners. What is particularly intriguing about this quote, as well as the entire collection of essays in the book, is that it was published in 1930, the year after the stock market crash, but more importantly, eighty-five years ago—essentially at the elbow of the above graphs, before our world completely sold out to our modern, industrial, progressivist culture.

This is the beauty of the wisdom of the great Distributists,[2] such as Orestes Brownson, G. K. Chesterton, and Hilaire Belloc, and later Monsignor Luigi G. Ligutti (author of *Rural Roads to Security*). Their writings give us a glimpse into what life was like just as the curve was beginning to accelerate upward, out-side of and before this modern culture in which most of us have always lived.

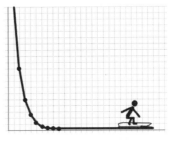

So now, eighty-five years later, as we ride the crest of this wave of progress, how do we respond? Some today are so enamored of—or dare I say, addicted to—the ever increasing

---

[1] Louis D. Rubin Jr., introduction to *I'll Take My Stand: The South and the Agrarian Tradition*, by Twelve Southerners (New York: Harper and Brothers, 1930), xxvi–xxvii.

[2] Distributism is an economic system that is centered on the widest possible ownership of property as the best guarantee of political and economic freedom. A family that owns its own land or its own tools can make its own way in the world without being dependent on someone else for a "job". Thus, Distributism, as opposed to socialism, communism, or capitalism, seeks to extend property ownership to as many as possible, and end the concentration of ownership by a few capitalists or state officials (a revised quote from *The Distributist Review*, http://distributistreview.com/mag/test-2/).

enticements of our modern, industrial, progressivist culture that their answer is to turn the graph on its side. They view this accelerating, ever changing, ever precarious economic culture as the inevitable trajectory of human ingenuity—human evolution—and, therefore, a thrilling blessing that must be freely embraced. They see no reason to question any of the demands of this culture; rather, they preach that we are to trust our futures to the trajectory of progress. Our sad present plight, however, is that none of the political parties vying for control of our government have anything to offer, except alternative ways to ride the accelerating economic wave.

The twelve southern agrarian authors quoted earlier, however, offer a different conclusion:

> If a community, or a section, or a race, or an age, is groaning under industrialism, and well aware that it is an evil dispensation, it must find the way to throw it off. To think that this cannot be done is pusillanimous. And if the whole community, section, race, or age thinks it cannot be done, then it has simply lost its political genius and doomed itself to impotence.[3]

Have we lost our political genius and doomed ourselves, and our children, to economic impotence?

As I sit on my back porch, finishing my drink of choice, seven (the biblical number of perfection) alternative steps come to mind.

1. Focus on the stable and established.

We should turn our focus away from the accelerating instability of our progressive culture and onto that which is stable and established. When we're riding the ever changing wave of economic progress, we can be dangerously comforted by the sight of thousands of others mindlessly riding along beside us. They coax us along, assuring us that there is nothing to fear ahead: "Surely economic growth and human ingenuity will prevail in the end, and, of course, doesn't God bless the *faithful*?" But in His Sermon on the Mount, Jesus told His followers to turn their focus away from the anxieties of their lives and onto "the birds of the air" and "the lilies of the field" (Mt 6:26, 28).

[3] Rubin, introduction, in Twelve Southerners, *I'll Take My Stand*, xxx.

To me, at the core of Distributist theory is the desire to make every effort to tie our lives and our families' lives to that which is stable and never changing, to that which has been there from the beginning and will always be there. Certainly, as baptized Christians, we are no longer citizens of this world, but mere sojourners, pilgrims here, passing through (see Eph 2:19). Jesus, however, did not take us immediately out of this world, but left us here to be witnesses to the  truth (see Jn 17:15). This world, which is our God-given way station on our journey toward our permanent home, was created good and for our enjoyment as well as our sustenance (see Jas 1:17). When we pause to look into the night sky at a star, we should consider that, regardless of the accelerating changes around us, that star has not changed in position in the constellations since it was created in love by our Father God; that star was in that location for every person who has ever lived.

Last night, as I crossed the yard from the house to the chicken house to shut the clucks in for the night, I glanced up at the clear night sky. Ursa Major was to my left, and further up to my right shone Jupiter. Scientific materialists will use every means available to study the stars, their origins and compositions, will use technology to get us closer and closer to them, but never in their lifetime, in a generation of lifetimes, will they discover the beauty and purpose of the stars and other celestial objects until they recognize that behind them all is the love of our Creator God for the highest in His creation, man. When young shepherd David sat on a hillside three thousand years ago tending his sheep, gazing upon Ursa Major and Jupiter, these gifts in the sky were doing the same thing that they should be doing for you and me today: drawing our thankful hearts upward to our loving Creator God. In awe, David wrote these words:

> When I look at your heavens, the work of your fingers,
>   the moon and the stars which you have established;
> what is man that you are mindful of him,
>   and the son of man that you care for him?

Yet you have made him little less than the angels,
  and you have crowned him with glory and honor.
You have given him dominion over the works of
    your hands;
  you have put all things under his feet,
all sheep and oxen,
  and also the beasts of the field,
the birds of the air, and the fish of the sea,
  whatever passes along the paths of the sea.
O LORD, our Lord,
  how majestic is your name in all the earth! (Ps 8:3–9)

One can also detect this stability through the patient study of nature and wildlife. With the constant, ever escalating changes around us, throughout history, through the rise and fall of cultures, empires, and civilizations, the animals and plants continue on, undaunted by any of this. Certainly their lives and existence, sometimes even their genetic composition, are affected by our care or our neglect, our conservation or our exploitation, yet God has granted them freedom from intellectual questions or concern. This is why God has given us the responsible stewardship of their needs. The chipmunks that feast on the spilled grain in my barn live out their lives in the stability and balance of nature, as their ancestors have done for hundreds of generations.

An even more powerful yet intimate means of growing in appreciation of that which is stable and established is to contemplate the mere flame of a candle. The most common object in nearly every religious sanctuary around the world is a candle, and the flames that burn on the wicks of these candles during worship have not changed since the creation of the world. In the privacy of your "prayer closet", light a candle and watch it. Anything else you might place before you in some way has been altered by man or beast, shaped, compounded, purged, or polluted, even a fistful of dirt, but this simple flame has always remained the same. It flickers and moves, as it consumes the wax and responds to the air in the room, even to one's motions, yet this mysterious flicker—but a spark of all the fires raging around the world—is a connection with all people who have ever warmed themselves, cooked, read, worshipped, or fellowshipped around a fire throughout history. It unites us with the stable and established, and it unites us with our Creator: "The LORD is my light and my salvation; whom shall I fear?" (Ps 27:1).

This first step gives us a solid handhold for the steps that follow.

2. Reduce the incessant voices.

We need to examine and subsequently reduce the incessant voices in our lives. Whom are we reading? To whom are we listening? What books, magazines, television shows, news broadcasts, blogs, Internet pundits, and radio commentators fill our every waking moment? Are they pulling us closer to God and independence  or enticing us to sell our souls along the accelerating path of economic progress and wealth? Are they encouraging us to trust our futures to the "certain" earnings of our investments, or are they helping us see that the more we detach ourselves from these vaporous promises, the freer we are to enjoy the blessings of the present moment?

A well-known comedian described the crisis he caused in his family when he listened to the radio broadcast of "The Chicken Heart That Ate Up New York City". His parents had left him home alone in his crib (a different time, a different world). Against his father's specific orders, he snuck out of his crib and turned on the scary radio program *Lights Out*. After he had become totally terrified by the loud thumping chicken heart, which the narrator said was coming down his street and was now standing outside his door, he spread Jell-O everywhere to slip up that monster! When his parents returned, hearing the loud thumping of the radio chicken heart, his father screamed, slipped, and nearly killed himself. When he asked his son what the @#$%& was going on, the boy screamed in terror, "The chicken heart's coming to eat us up!" His father's solution? He turned the radio off! In the sudden, still silence of their home, the boy admitted sheepishly, "I never thought of that."

How many of the voices in our lives do we merely need to turn off in order to make true progress toward the stability and peace that God promises? Dorothy Day said it well seventy-three years ago in her journal, as related by Paul Elite: " 'Turn off your radio, put away your daily paper. Read one review of events a week and spend time reading.' Life would go on; other people would continue to 'eat, sleep, love, worship, marry, have children, and somehow live in the midst of war, in the midst of anguish.' Herself, she would pray, work, and read novels."[4]

Recently, I was driving through a pleasant small village in central Ohio. At the one stoplight, I pulled to a stop. The intersection was a beautifully preserved portrait of nostalgic rural America. Across the way, in a small, immaculately tended park honoring the town's Civil War veterans, a grove of two-hundred-year-old maples and oaks was afire in fall foliage. Under their boughs, a teenage girl passed. She walked briskly, face down, earbuds implanted, her attention solely on the smartphone in her hand, her fingers working intently in textual conversation with someone not there. She reached the corner, glanced up just enough to see the confirmation of the lighted man on the crosswalk sign, then regained her gait and returned to her conversation. She continued across the intersection, up onto the next curb, and then out of my sight. She had not noticed or demonstrated any concern for anything around her. When I was young, in those innocent days before earbuds, Walkmans, or even transistor radios, I would have had little to distract me from those surroundings. I might have been kicking a can or chucking a stone, but I'm sure I would have been at least a little curious about, maybe even a bit observant of, the park, the statue of the Union soldier, the cascading red leaves, and the squirrels scurrying frantically in preparation for winter. But this modern teenage girl wasn't really *there*; she was miles away, and the park and its symbols were inconsequential.

We need to silence those earbuds as we walk through nature so we can appreciate the magnificent beauty, as well as the inspiring symphony of the crickets and birds.

3. Reduce financial entanglements.

I strongly suggest making what some might consider radical changes in your financial entanglements. Nothing ties us as individuals, as

---

[4] Quoted in Paul Elite, *The Life You Save May Be Your Own* (New York: Farrar, Straus and Giroux, 2003), 117.

families, and as a nation to the accelerating grip of our changing economic culture than our debts and our investments. The more we can get out of debt and, as the good Distributists have been telling us for years, situated securely on our own piece of land with our own home, no matter how small and meager, the more we can become detached from the effects of any craziness that might occur in our nation or world. Even if all the markets rebound, and our friends wag their fingers that we were foolish not to have placed all our eggs in the  basket of progress, they actually have only moved one minute step halfway toward an unreachable goal of "increasing disadjustment and instability". As I write this, one month ago the stock market had reached an all-time high—now, it has dropped a thousand points, vacillating three hundred points up or down every day.

Last spring, I left our rural land to drive into a large city that was surrounded by seemingly endless housing developments. It reminded me of the myth propagated in the mass media about overpopulation. All anyone needs to do is fly cross-country and see the endless miles of unpopulated territory to recognize that the true problem isn't overpopulation. Rather, the true problem arises from what was assumed, for example, by all the candidates in all the parties in all the primaries of the 2012 presidential election: that every American should have the opportunity to attain the American dream; every American should be able to become a member of the "middle class" (in this supposedly classless culture). I will discuss this in more detail in a later chapter, but the more we—as individuals, families, and a culture—define the American dream as the accumulation of more and more things (which requires more and more money), the more we have set our families and culture on an unsustainable death spiral toward political and economic chaos. On this trajectory, the poverty level is continually redefined upward, and the expectations and "rights" increase proportionately. As a result, government subsidies and entitlement programs must increase—as of this writing, nearly one third of the American population is living on government assistance. On this trajectory and under these assumptions, abortion, contraception, euthanasia, along with mood-altering drugs, and even the endorsement of relationships that produce fewer children become the necessary tools of those in power to control the population so that more and more can rise to the material level of the "middle class". In this quest, our government has amassed a 18.2-trillion-dollar deficit, increasing at an exponential rate, all to satisfy a material-hungry populace. Who will pay for this? Not us, for Pilate-like, we wash our hands of all guilt and pass on to the grave, leaving the payment to our children and grandchildren. (Does anyone really have a workable solution to our national debt? As I write this, the population of the United States is 320,673,933, so it is estimated that each citizen's share of that debt is $56,619.74![5])

The only solution is for all in America, from the top down, to seek satisfaction with less; not just for the "haves" to share their wealth with the "have-nots", but for the entire "American dream" to be redefined on a more realistic, sustainable scale. I have little hope that this will happen in America, for the last half of the last century was all about raising the expectations of everyone's right to financial progress and independence. Once this toothpaste is out of the tube, it's impossible to put it back, short of a resetting of expectations through a major worldwide crisis, such as a depression or war, or through pervasive conversions of heart. There is little we can do to stop any of this, except as individuals and families to consider, as I said at the beginning of this section, "radical changes in [our] financial entanglements".

One of the previously mentioned southern agrarians wrote in his essay "The Philosophy of Progress", again in 1930:

> One outstanding fact in industry at present is that with the great increase in production and in new commodities, and with consumption coerced to the limit, there is a steady decrease in employment. Improvement in technology, as Mr. Stuart Chase has recently pointed out, "can mean only one thing. An equivalent tonnage of goods can be produced by a declining number of workers, and men must lose their jobs by the thousands—presently by the millions."[6]

This author was writing at the elbow of the curve, but we, eighty-five years later, have only "progressed" further along the trajectory

---

[5] From the U.S. National Debt Clock, http://www.brillig.com/debt_clock.
[6] Lyle H. Lanier, "Critique of the Philosophy of Progress", in *I'll Take My Stand*, 149.

of his warnings. He had no idea how prophetic he was, for a couple of paragraphs later he commented, "Another world war, which the international struggle for markets suggests as not an unlikely prospect, would afford temporary relief."[7] World War II, coming eleven years later, did indeed provide some temporary "relief", but the industrialization that ensued has never waned, nor has the escalating national debt or the oscillating unemployment. What major "relief" is around the bend in our future?

Even one of the most influential players in our modern, industrial, progressivist culture, Bill Gates, admits that accelerating technologies, many of which he had a hand in developing, will drastically change the work environment even more for our children and grandchildren. Speaking at the American Enterprise Institute in Washington, D.C., he said, "Software substitution, whether it's for drivers or waiters or nurses ... [is] progressing.... Technology over time will reduce demand for jobs, particularly at the lower end of skill set.... *Twenty years from now, labor demand for lots of skill sets will be substantially lower.* I don't think people have that in their mental model."[8]

The more we can detach ourselves, adopting what our Lord called a "poverty of spirit" (cf. Mt 5:3), from the attachments to the world beckoning us from every side, the more we can grow in the next step.

4. Practice personal subsidiarity.

I believe an amazing sense of freedom comes from practicing personal subsidiarity. In his introduction to *Flee to the Fields: The Faith and Works of the Catholic Land Movement*, Dr. Tobias Lanz gave the following helpful definition of social subsidiarity:

> Social subsidiarity ... holds that an individual should rely on the most basic levels of social and technical complexity to achieve his goals. Higher levels are called upon only when the lower echelon is insufficient to the task. Thus, by relying on the household, family,

---

[7] Ibid., 150.

[8] Rick Moran, "Gates: Software to Replace Millions of Human Jobs in 20 Years", *American Thinker*, March 15, 2014, http://www.americanthinker.com/blog/2014/03/gates_software _to_replace_millions_of_human_jobs_in_20_years.html.

community, and nature's bounty to provide as many basic needs as possible, people could free themselves from economic dependence and the political control of the plutocrats, and thereby regain a modicum of human dignity and freedom.[9]

Applying this in personal practice, we can examine how we spend our money, where we place our investments, where we shop, and where we purchase our goods, beginning first close to home and only then working outward.

Our little central-Ohio village, initially a thriving canal town, then a farm community, and then the location of a nationally known manufacturer of handmade baskets, now sits in many ways like a ghost town. Nine out of ten stores sit vacant.

Why? Because, over time, all the long-standing, family-owned and -operated specialty shops that had provided the community with their bodily needs and more could not compete with the strip malls selling transported American goods at cheaper prices. The strip malls were then supplanted by the super and mega stores selling imported international goods at even cheaper prices, and these have now been supplanted by Internet stores, which not only sell but originate from all around the globe, selling everything at even cheaper prices. How can anyone consider opening a small local store in our little backwoods village when anything any villager might want to grow, make, or sell can be purchased cheaper not just from a local mall but from the convenience of a home desktop computer? The question to ask yourself when you pick up the phone to order a pizza is this: Will your payment remain to some extent in your community, supporting a local family, or will it mostly pass out of your community into the hands of a corporation in some other city, state, or even country? The more we can focus our lives locally, from our families to our communities, supporting the efforts of our neighbors, the more we can contribute to the security of our local economies.

[9] Dr. Tobias Lanz, *Flee to the Fields: The Faith and Works of the Catholic Land Movement* (Norfolk, Va.: IHS Press, 2003), 8.

5. Live more simply.

I am hardly the first voice in the past two thousand years of Christianity to suggest that a life in the footsteps of Christ is a life of simplicity. This has been the constant message of the Church and the saints, as well as spiritual writers throughout the ages, ever since our Lord made this the centerpiece of His New Law, His Sermon on the Mount. So, to that extent, I hardly need to reiterate this, except maybe to emphasize that this is always a relative  move—relative to one's present state of life and to where we are at the present moment: Are our goals or objectives, our labor, plans, investments, and dreams all leading away from or toward a life of simplicity? Or are they in complicity with our culture, driven by self-promotion, consumption, accumulation, and hoarding?

Early on, the apostle Paul warned his congregations to beware of the constant call away from the pure, simple gospel of Christ: "But I fear, lest by any means, as the serpent beguiled Eve through his subtlety, so your minds should be corrupted from the simplicity that is in Christ" (2 Cor 11:3, KJV). Indeed, the voices of temptation bombarding us from every direction are very subtle, and it is particularly interesting to note just how accurately the first graph in this chapter depicts the agelong battle of the enemy against simplicity. It has always been gradual and subtle, relying on the means and technologies of each age. Today, however, the call away from simplicity toward progress is so relentless that the mere suggestion of choosing a simpler life is a dangerous clarion cry of treason against our American right of upward mobility and the pursuit of the "American dream".

Andrew Nelson Lytle, in his contribution to *I'll Take My Stand*, made this challenge to agrarians, in 1930, to return to a simpler life:

> To avoid the dire consequences and to maintain a farming life in an industrial imperialism, there seems to be only one thing left for the farmer to do, and particularly for the small farmer. Until he

and the agrarian West and all the conservative communities throughout the United States can unite on some common political action,
he must deny himself the articles the industrialists offer for sale. It is
not so impossible as it may seem at first, for, after all, the necessities
they machine-facture were once manufactured on the land, and as
for the bric-a-brac, let it rot on their hands. Do what we did after the
war [the Civil War] and the Reconstruction: return to our looms,
our handcrafts, our reproducing stock. Throw out the radio and take
down the fiddle from the wall. Forsake the movies for the play-parties
and the square dances. And turn away from the liberal capons who
fill the pulpits as preachers. Seek a priesthood that may manifest the
will and intelligence to renounce science and search out the Word in
the authorities.[10]

The economist E. F. Schumacher is best known for his seminal
work, *Small Is Beautiful*.[11] Much of what he wrote and believed is
applicable to almost everything I'm trying to say in this book. I'd like
to draw attention, though, to his article "Technology and Political
Change", written in 1976, five years after his conversion to the Catholic faith. Schumacher wrote:

> As our modern society is unquestionably in crisis, there must
> be something that does not fit: (a) If overall performance is poor
> despite brilliant technology, maybe the "system" does not fit. (b) Or
> maybe the technology itself does not fit present-day realities, includ-
> ing human nature.... I never cease to be astonished at the docility
> with which people—even those who call themselves Socialists or
> Marxists—accept technology, uncritically, as if technology were a
> part of Natural Law.[12]

In other words, for centuries people have blamed the problems in the
world on the governmental and political systems, whether communist, socialist, Marxist, democratic, capitalist, libertarian, or what have
you, while always presuming that the rising technologies in all these
systems were good and beyond blame.

[10] Andrew Nelson Lytle, "The Hind Tit", in *I'll Take My Stand*, 244.
[11] E. F. Shumacher, *Small Is Beautiful* (1973; repr., New York: Harper Perennial, 2010).
Also, see Joseph Pearce's insightful review and reflection on this book, *Small Is Still Beautiful:
Economics as if Families Mattered* (Wilmington, Del.: Intercollegiate Studies Institute, 2006).
[12] E. F. Schumacher, "Technology and Political Change", in *This I Believe and Other Essays*
(Devon, United Kingdom: Resurgence Books, 1998), 98–99.

Schumacher continued:

> People still say: it is not the technology; it is the "system". Maybe a particular "system" gave birth to this technology; but now it stares us in the face that the system we have is the product, the inevitable product of the technology. As I compare the societies which appear to have different "systems", the evidence seems to be overwhelming that where they employ the same technology they act very much the same and become more alike every day. Mindless work in office or factory is equally mindless under any system.
>
> I suggest therefore that those who want to promote a better society, achieve a better system, must not confine their activities to attempts to change the "superstructure"—laws, rules, agreements, taxes, welfare, education, health services, etc. The expenditure incurred in trying to buy a better society can be like pouring money into a bottomless pit. If there is no change in the base—which is technology—there is unlikely to be any real change in the superstructure.[13]

What I consider particularly astounding about these comments is that they were said at the elbow of the graph, before our modern lives became irrevocably entrenched in addictive technologies. In 1976, when Schumacher wrote, there were no personal or laptop computers; no cell phones or smartphones; no iPads, iPods, or even Walkmans (which were first released in 1978); no cable or 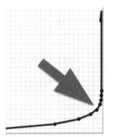 satellite television; no e-mails or texting; no social networks; no Nintendo, Xbox, or PlayStation; there were none of these technologies that demand our regular subscriptions, upgrades, syncing, and constant attention.

Back in 1976, if Schumacher had unplugged his landline telephone or left his home, he would have been living in a world in which he was essentially unreachable, and free. Can any of us go a month, a week, or even a day without any of these addictive technologies? The question is, are we better and holier people with these technologies, or because of them? Has our culture become more wholesome and godly through the growth of these technologies? If not, is it the system, politics, ideologies, and superstructure of our culture that is the

---

[13] Ibid., 100.

problem? Schumacher would say it isn't the system—it is the technologies that have enticed, captured, and carried us away.

Consider this. Recently in Rome the Catholic Church held an extraordinary synod on the family. As never before in history, the world could follow nearly every word and every debate of every committee of bishops, and the commentaries flowed and frothed freely. Progressives of every stripe hoped the Church would change her centuries-old unaltered views on marriage, divorce, remarriage, homosexuality, and gay marriage, and conservatives feared that cultural momentum would carry the day. In the midst of this worldwide coverage, a Catholic LGBT (lesbian, gay, bisexual, and transgender) group announced that it had initiated a lobbying effort to influence eight of the most conservative bishops in America. Its literature indicated that these target bishops were the "most outspoken in their rejection of LGBT Catholics, their civil rights, and their rightful place in the church". There is much that I found troubling about the lobbying assumptions and efforts of this group, but the most enigmatic information that emerged was that the corporate partners of this group were "large corporations like American Airlines, Apple, Google, Microsoft, Bank of America, Northrop Grumman, Chevron, Lexus, Goldman Sachs, Coca-Cola and PepsiCo."[14] When I read this article I was flying on American Airlines; I was reading it on an Apple computer; I had used Google to find the article; at least half of the software on my computer is made by Microsoft; some of the investments that paid for my trip are in Bank of America; the plane in which I was flying likely had parts manufactured by Northrop Grumman; I bought gas for my pickup at the Chevron station near the airport; I've lusted over buying a Lexus; the fingers of Goldman Sachs are everywhere; and throughout my trip I've quaffed many a Diet Coke, or Diet Pepsi if Coke wasn't available. All I do is provide funds for this LGBT lobbyist group!

How do we extricate ourselves from this web of finances? Is it even possible anymore? If it is the devil's goal to convince the world

[14] Kevin Jones, "LGBT Activist Group Hopes to Influence Family Synod", October 15, 2014, *Catholic News Agency*, http://www.catholicnewsagency.com/news/lgbt-activist-group -hopes-to-influence-family-synod-43386/.

to become tolerant of every conceivable lifestyle, this will require the attacks of many lobbying groups from many fronts. Besides the devilish whisper that every person hears in his inner mind, these groups need lots and lots of money. How better to fund their lobbying than by providing technologies to which the world becomes so addicted that they can no longer imagine living without. Thousands of people lined up all night long to be the first to own the new iPhone 6, when there really was nothing essentially wrong with the iPhone 5 or 4 or any of the previous models, or even the most basic of cell phones. Have the technologies enticed, captured, and carried us away?

Today nearly every dollar we spend goes to companies, particularly technology companies, that use our money to promote lifestyles we may consider immoral or are contrary to the values of our faith. To what extent are we culpable for this funding, particularly if we have come to know about a corporation's spending practices?

I can hear in my mind the voices even of friends who belittle my concerns. They merely respond, "It has always been this way—even the first-century Christians had to pay tax to Rome! And besides, it would be impossible to extricate yourself—you'd have to quit buying anything!"

But has it always been what it is today? I recently did an experiment that probably anyone my age could do. When I was four, in the midfifties, my parents had low-level management jobs with the telephone company. My father had worked his way up from an installer to a supervisor, and my mother had risen from an operator to an engineer—both without college. My father had just completed building our home, from a Sears and Roebuck kit, on a half-acre lot in our small northwestern Ohio town.

With a little reflection, I think I've come up with a pretty good guess at what their expenses were:

- mortgage with local bank
- Ford car loan with local bank
- gas and car maintenance through local gas station
- electric, gas, waste, phone, and water service through local companies
- a television set that received five free local stations
- a radio that received about ten free local stations

- a subscription to the local newspaper
- federal, state, and local taxes, and social security and Medicare costs
- groceries from our local family-owned market

Both had retirement plans provided by their employer. I don't think they had health insurance; we went to the doctor's office only for crisis care; otherwise, the doctor made house calls.

Now, I am quite certain that back in the fifties none of the national or local companies to which my parents were paying money were funneling funds to promote lifestyles contrary to their beliefs; these corporations were not yet funding action groups promoting abortion, contraception, euthanasia, guns for terrorists, or same-sex marriage. And none of these companies were being run by people who were openly promoting any of these issues. Certainly some of these corporate leaders may have been philanderers, adulterers, or thieves—but they were not openly advocating these lifestyles, and if they were caught committing immoral acts, they were generally ostracized, fired, and sometimes prosecuted. It never even crossed my parents' minds that any of these companies would be contributing to organizations promoting alternative lifestyles. They would have been shocked to discover this—as they became appalled as these lifestyles became more and more accepted, and then promoted, in our culture.

Today nearly every one of these companies is somehow invested in promoting alternative lifestyles and values, either directly or indirectly, and often blatantly so. And particularly, these corporations are providing the very technological entertainment and networking services to which we as a culture have become dependent—dare I say, addicted.

What is most striking about this is that it has all happened within my lifetime, from the elbow to the near vertical ascent of that graph. What will our culture be like for my children and grandchildren? We are drowning in this soup, and it seems beyond our capabilities to divest ourselves of any of this. And the devil laughs.

I can still sense many complaining about such an uncalled-for attack on these technologies, which have become so pervasive and necessary in our twenty-first-century lives. But Jesus made a far bolder attack on the lifestyle of His first-century audience:

If your right eye causes you to sin, pluck it out and throw it away; it is better that you lose one of your members than that your whole body be thrown into hell. And if your right hand causes you to sin, cut it off and throw it away; it is better that you lose one of your members than that your whole body go into hell. (Mt 5:29–30)

Why would Jesus make such brash statements to those He was trying to attract as disciples? He was using hyperbole to drive home to His simple audience how serious He was about the central issue of all His teaching: "You, therefore, must be perfect, as your heavenly Father is perfect" (Mt 5:48). Theologians throughout the ages have tried to simplify, clarify, justify, and soften this statement, but the bottom line is, as emphasized later by Saint Paul, that we are called to be holy: "Since we have these promises, beloved, let us cleanse ourselves from every defilement of body and spirit, and make holiness perfect in the fear of God" (2 Cor 7:1).

If Jesus emphasized that what we do with our hands and what we look at with our eyes is crucial to our growth in holiness, and consequently our relationship with Him, shouldn't we be just as vigilant now with what we hold in our hands, put before our eyes, or plug into our ears?

Every step we take, even a small one, to simplify our lives—to examine critically how addicted we have become, especially to communicative technologies—is an effort to get in step with our Lord. Every step in rebellion against the marketeers who claim that happiness comes only with the accumulation of unnecessary stuff, and against the politicians who warn that the salvation of our economy and the "world as we know it" depends on this, is a step toward freedom from the frantic clutches of today's modern, industrial, progressivist culture.

6. Consider a more self-sufficient life on the land.

Steps 1 through 5 are all in line with the teachings of our Lord and His Church, and, admittedly, each requires willful sacrifice, empowered by grace. Step 6, however, is only for "those to whom this has been given". This is what Jesus said about those of His followers

called to the celibate life (see
Mt 19:11–12). The same is true,
though, for those called to live
a self-sufficient life on the land.
I hesitate to include this in the
list, because, indeed, not all are
called to this; maybe only a few.
There was a time, though, back
down and along the steep curve
of that graph, when the major-
ity of people in this world were self-sufficient or at least trying to
be. They admittedly led a simpler life with no thoughts or interest
in upward mobility. As Andrew Nelson Lytle wrote, "A farm is not
a place to grow wealthy; it is a place to grow corn."[15] It is a place
slowly, over time, to become free. Lytle continued his challenge to
those called to an agrarian life:

> Any man who grows his own food, kills his own meat, takes wool
> from his lambs and cotton from his stalks and makes them into clothes,
> plants corn and hay for his stock, shoes them at the crossroads black-
> smith shop, draws milk and butter from his cows, eggs from his pul-
> lets, water from the ground, and fuel from the woodlot, can live in
> an industrial world without a great deal of cash. Let him diversify, but
> diversify so that he may live rather than that he may grow rich.[16]

As mentioned earlier in this chapter, Monsignor Luigi G. Ligutti
made much the same claims, exactly ten years later, in his important
book *Rural Roads to Security: America's Third Struggle for Freedom*.
Monsignor Ligutti, the executive secretary of the National Catholic
Rural Life Conference from 1940 through 1959, was the "unques-
tioned leader of the Catholic rural life movement".[17] There is far
too much good stuff in his book to quote here, so let one long
quote suffice:

---

[15] Lytle, "The Hind Tit", in *I'll Take My Stand*, 205.

[16] Ibid., 244.

[17] David S. Bovee, *The Church and the Land: The National Catholic Rural Life Conference and American Society, 1923–2007* (Washington, D.C.: The Catholic University of America Press, 2010), 153.

To have economic independence a man must be in a position to leave one job and go to another; he must have enough savings of some kind to exist for a considerable time without accepting the first job offered. Thus the peasant, for all his poverty and the exploitation which he suffers, is relative to his own needs still the freest man in central Europe. The fact that he can exist by his own labor on his own piece of land gives him an independence which every dictatorial regime, except the Russian perhaps, has been forced to respect.

But the industrial worker who has a choice between working in one factory and not working at all, the white collar intellectuals who compete savagely for the relatively few private positions and posts in the bureaucracy—these are the people who live too precariously to exercise their liberties or to defend them. They have no savings. They have only their labor to sell, and there are very few buyers of their labor.

The more I see of Europe the more deeply convinced do I become that the preservation of freedom in America, or anywhere else, depends upon maintaining and restoring for the great majority of individuals the economic means to remain independent individuals. The greatest evil of the modern world is the reduction of the people to a proletarian level by destroying their savings, by depriving them of private property, by making them the helpless employees of private monopoly or of government monopoly. At that point they are no longer citizens. They are a mob.[18]

In his book, Monsignor Ligutti offered many hopeful and practical suggestions on helping the poor gain dignity. Instead of putting the poor and unemployed on welfare and food stamps—which too often, even to this day, encourages many to lose their desire to better themselves and seek employment—he outlined a quite workable plan to help the poor become self-sufficient homesteaders on their own small piece of land. Before his proposal could barely be tested, however, his book was shelved and forgotten, because, in the next year came Pearl Harbor, and the "relief" that was prophesied by that earlier southern agrarian writer.

The hope and practical solutions of Monsignor Ligutti still hold true, however, and given the fulfillment of so many of the Distributist warnings of the 1930s and '40s—and at an acceleration that none of

[18] Rt. Rev. Msgr. Luigi G. Ligutti, *Rural Roads to Security: America's Third Struggle for Freedom* (Milwaukee: Bruce Publishing, 1940), 20.

them could have imagined—the challenge is still extended to any of us "to whom this has been given" to follow our vocation to self-sufficient simplicity.

At this point, some readers might be wondering whether I consider myself one of those "to whom this has been given". I can't deny that, even in the time it has taken to write and rewrite this book, I have struggled over this question. And maybe by the time this book has landed in your hands, I will have been led to a different conclusion.

What I have come to realize is how much this is more a corporate than an individual decision. If you are an individual hermit, with few, if any, attachments, you are free to discern for yourself and initiate all the radical changes necessary to live a self-sufficient life off the grid. But, just as with the advice given by Christ in Matthew 19, if you are married and have children and grandchildren, the permutations of attachments and responsibilities make these kinds of countercultural changes exponentially more difficult—specifically the means of discerning God's call to this vocation.

As for Marilyn and me, we have progressed an amazing distance down the road of self-sufficiency, but extended family and other responsibilities, as well as my own waffling convictions, leave the trajectory of our self-sufficiency in the hands of God.

7. Make more time for God.

Given all the changes suggested above, we can now focus on that which is most import-ant: make more time to talk with and listen to God. Not that we should wait until we've completed the first six steps before embarking on the seventh—far from it! Rather, making time for Him is our perennial duty, and the previous six steps can facilitate this. By focus-ing on that which is more stable, and not forever moving and elusive; by shutting our 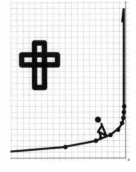 minds to the thousands of conflicting, clamoring voices around us; by freeing ourselves from the clutching control and anxieties of debt and unsure investments; by investing our lives in the immediate world around us, the specific world in which God has planted us; by choosing to make steps toward a life of gospel simplicity; and, for those "to whom this has been given", by seeking a life of self-sufficiency on one's own piece of land, we can become freer to commune with God in prayer, to meditate on His Word in Scripture, to hear His voice in liturgy, and to receive His grace and forgiveness—His very self—in the sacraments. We can become freer to recognize the fingerprints of His love in nature, and to more effectively become the persons He created in His image.

Saint Paul promised, "Have no anxiety about anything, but in everything by prayer and supplication with thanksgiving let your requests be made known to God. And the peace of God, which passes all understanding, will keep your hearts and your minds in Christ Jesus" (Phil 4:6–7).

As I prepare to retire from our back porch for the night, I think it's important to conclude this chapter with a disclaimer; in fact, the same one that Saint Paul gave: "Not that I have already obtained this or am already perfect; but I press on to make it my own, because Christ Jesus has made me his own" (Phil 3:12). I am certainly far from completing any of these seven steps, particularly the last, but my wife and I together have come to believe that these are important goals for us as a family. So pray for us, and we will pray for you.

Frogs in the Soup, Unite: Jump Out!

*Thus says the LORD: "Let not the wise man glory in his
wisdom, let not the mighty man glory in his might, let
not the rich man glory in his riches; but let him who glo-
ries glory in this, that he understands and knows me, that
I am the LORD who practice steadfast love, justice, and
righteousness in the earth; for in these things I delight,
says the LORD."*

—Jeremiah 9:23–24

Certainly the history behind this little pinprick on the globe that
God has given my family to care for is of interest to few beyond our
immediate family. But where our hundred-year-old barn sits is the
location of the original settler's log cabin. It seems he chose this spot,
miles from the nearest settlement, because it was in the Y between
two converging creeks, each originating farther uphill from two natural springs. In fact, our hilly land is burgeoning with springs.

Not long after we moved in, we noticed that a small section of the
land uphill from the barn was always damp. My sons and I decided
to determine why and, in our digging, discovered yet another spring.
As water seeped from the hillside, a crayfish poked out its head from
the mud, which I was told was a grand sign of a good clean spring!
Further digging revealed, to our ecstatic surprise, a long-buried,
thirty-foot length of hand-hewn wooden trough that must have once
guided water from this spring down to the house for the family or
the livestock.

We too needed to get water out to the barn, so we hired an exca-
vator, who developed this ancient spring into a four-season natural
water supply for the barn as well as a year-round stock tank for our

critters. Cattle, sheep, and a swaybacked horse have gratefully quaffed at this tank, but it has also become the home for a school of goldfish and a mess of frogs.

The morning after I had written the first draft of the previous chapter, I was feeling sheepish about whether I ought to release these words into the public forum. But then, in my devotions, I happened to read the eleventh chapter of Sirach (aka Ecclesiasticus or the Wisdom of Jesus the son of Sirach) and found that the author was affirming  everything I had tried to say. With self-congratulatory glee, I headed out to the barn for my morning chores, and there, sitting on the stock tank, greeting me with a cynical sneer, was one of our freeloading frogs. And this all made me think.

Never in the history of mankind has the proverbial image comparing society to frogs in a soup pot been more apropos. You know the old analogy about how to cook a frog? If you drop him into a pot of boiling water, he'll immediately know it's "too hot for comfort" and jump out. But if you first drop the frog into a pot of unheated water, he'll contentedly swim around, not noticing as you gradually raise the temperature, while he cheerfully, though unknowingly, becomes frog soup.

The vociferous voices inundating us with advice on how to live our lives—and particularly how to plan our financial futures as we struggle along the ascending slope of our modern, industrial, progressivist, relativist culture—are excruciatingly contradictory, yet also blindly comforting. Imagine yourself a frog swimming in an immense soup pot with a thousand other frogs, all croaking at the same time: that's the garrulous guidance coming at us from all sides through the media. It's tempting to surrender and say, "With such confident croaking, they must know more than I do about financial matters! So I'll just keep swimming along in this vat with everybody else."

Maybe the Lord, however, is calling us to do something different— maybe even to shock everyone, especially our portfolio managers— and not just swim against the stream, but jump out of that pot! In fact, isn't this exactly what our Lord called us all to do, when He said:

Do not lay up for yourselves treasures on earth, where moth and rust consume and where thieves break in and steal, but lay up for yourselves treasures in heaven, where neither moth nor rust consumes and where thieves do not break in and steal. For where your treasure is, there will your heart be also.

The eye is the lamp of the body. So, if your eye is sound, your whole body will be full of light; but if your eye is not sound, your whole body will be full of darkness. If then the light in you is darkness, how great is the darkness!

No one can serve two masters; for either he will hate the one and love the other, or he will be devoted to the one and despise the other. You cannot serve God and mammon. (Mt 6:19–24)

What kind of treasure are the voices around us in this soup vat encouraging us to lay up? Are those voices placing before our eyes light or darkness? And whom are they calling us to serve?

Before some of us end up facing a foreclosure or a Chapter 11 (or 7 or 13) bankruptcy, maybe we can learn something from the wisdom in chapter 11 of Sirach. Some of you might be thinking, "Wait a second: Sirach isn't in my Bible! Why should I listen to him?" But as Sirach suggests:

> Do not find fault before you investigate;
>   first consider, and then reprove.
> Do not answer before you have heard,
>   nor interrupt a speaker in the midst of his words.
>   (Sir 11:7–8)

As far as we can tell from historical documents, the first official definition of the canon (i.e., contents) of Holy Scripture was recorded in A.D. 382. There were earlier lists—some longer and others shorter; some that rejected books that eventually would be included and others that included books that eventually would be rejected—but this canon, which became the standard for all Bibles for over a thousand years, was confirmed, not merely by a random gathering of well-meaning Christian ministers, but by a council of Catholic bishops gathered under Pope Damasus I in Rome. Before this canon was shortened by the sixteenth-century Reformers, it included all the books presently in Catholic and Orthodox Bibles (as well as the original edition of the King James Bible). The preserved report from the council specifically includes, as a part of the divine Scriptures, "Ecclesiasticus, one book".[1]

Even though the Protestant Reformers did not include this book in their canon, they did consider it good spiritual reading. So, it might behoove us at least "first [to] consider, and ... [not] interrupt a speaker in the midst of his words". What I find challenging, though, is how pertinent to our day is the wisdom of this "Jesus, the son of Sirach" who wrote two or three hundred years before Jesus Christ our Savior lived on this earth. There is much in the entire book worth reading, but here are just a few thoughts.

Busy, Busy, Busy!

We live in a frenzied age, driven by the false assumption of "progress" and the all-powerful saving grace of "human ingenuity". From an early age, most of us have been preparing for a place on the ladder of upward mobility, many times only to find ourselves in a treadwheel instead. On this laborious apparatus—just a larger version of the exercise wheel our hamsters so mindlessly enjoy—leading nowhere, however, the words of our Lord, "[D]o not be anxious about your life" (Mt 6:25), make little sense. To this, the words of Sirach pose a prophetic warning:

> My son, do not busy yourself with many matters;
>   if you multiply activities you will not go unpunished;
> and if you pursue you will not overtake,
>   and by fleeing you will not escape. (Sir 11:10)

We will all one day answer to our Creator for what Sirach called the "many matters" with which we have "busied" ourselves. As Saint

---

[1] The entire report from the Council of Rome, as well as the canon, can be found at http://denzinger.patristica.net/; for further study, see Gary Michuta's books *Why Are Catholic Bibles Bigger* (Port Huron, Mich.: Grotto Press, 2013) and *The Case for the Deuterocanon: Evidence and Arguments* (Livonia, Mich.: Nikaria Press, 2015).

Paul wrote to the Christians of the Church of Corinth: "[W]e must all appear before the judgment seat of Christ, so that each one may receive good or evil, according to what he has done in the body" (2 Cor 5:10).

In the frenzied soup in which we live, we are barraged by the incessant croaking of the voices around us, tempting us to "multiply" our "activities", and at such decibels that it becomes nearly impossible to hear the beckoning of God. How can we "pray without ceasing" when we are doing everything else "without ceasing"?

In the book of Revelation, our Lord told the apostle John to warn the seven churches, "He who has an ear, let him hear what the Spirit says" (2:29). To five of those churches, He said, "I know your works", to another, "I know where you dwell", and to another, "I know your tribulation" (2:2ff.). In each case, however, He gave promises of future and eternal blessings to those who "conquer".

God knows our lives as well as our tribulations, and He promises, through His grace, to help us conquer—if we are willing to trust Him, even if following Him means jumping out of the pot of "progress and upward mobility".

Consequently, per the advice of Sirach, we must ask ourselves: In what ways do we need to curb our busyness "with many matters" and "activities" so that we can more readily hear, see, and follow God?

The Ambitious and the Simple

Our modern culture can also be likened to a swift flowing river (maybe even at the precipice of a waterfall!). Once we find ourselves being pulled along by the exhilarating current of "progress", it's next to impossible just to break from the flow, let alone get out of the river—especially when "expert" frog advisers warn us not only to stay in but to keep pressing forward. "And if you do flee," they warn, "you will regret it when the markets and the economy rebound!"

The goal of financial and family security based on the anticipation of escalating wages, compounded interest, and accumulated wealth, especially in our present volatile economy, is forever elusive (per that commercial we've all seen on television: "Is a 'gazillion' even enough?") because at the core, there is a fine line between trust in God and trust in the anticipated trajectory of wealth.

It's not merely that we are never satisfied, but also that the path of upward mobility places us alongside others likewise toiling and pressing on, pulling us forward. The problem is, there is that *other* tempting whisper—of the Deceiver—who tells us that we now deserve and really need to have what they have: "You've earned it!"

For you see, this crowded progressive river in which we are frantically swimming is far from homogenized, but is striated into intercommunicating, competing, if not combative, currents. Traditionally, these contiguous streams have been delineated between the rich and the poor, the haves and the have-nots, or the ambitious and the lazy; or, in today's political terms, the upper, middle, and lower "classes". From a different perspective—the perspective of how industrialism has affected our more traditional agrarian lifestyle—rural-life apologist Wendell Berry differentiated between the "unsettled" and the "settled".

Perhaps another way to describe the crosscurrents in this turbulent river is between those who are driven to accumulate more and more of this world's "treasures" and those who either choose or are gifted from above with the desire to live a simpler life of less and less. Sirach draws the distinction by describing the person who is driven to accumulate more and more as "a man who works, and toils, and presses on, but is so much the more in want" (11:11). Our Lord also built on this in His parable about a rich man who had accumulated so much that (instead of even considering sharing with his neighbors) he decided to replace his small barns with bigger ones to provide for his own future. The punch line to our Lord's parable, however, was this: "But God said to him, 'Fool! This night your soul is required of you; and the things you have prepared, whose will they be?' So is he who lays up treasure for himself, and is not rich toward God" (Lk 12:20–21).

Why are we working? I don't mean to suggest that we shouldn't be, but when we work, and as we're working, *why are we working*? Only to make more and more money to buy more and more things? Or to pay off the debts from buying more and more things?

Or to accumulate more and more so that one day we can comfortably quit working? Or maybe because it's the only job we can get right now, until the right or better job comes along?

All of these are good enough goals, but have you ever noticed that as we're pulled along in this frenetic current, as we work, toil, and press forward, we always find ourselves and our families so much the more in want?

Sirach further describes the ambitious in this way: "There is a man who is rich through his diligence and self-denial, and this is the reward allotted to him: when he says, 'I have found rest, and now I shall enjoy my goods!' he does not know how much time will pass until he leaves them to others and dies" (11:18–19).

Much "diligence and self-denial" are indeed necessary if one is to dedicate every effort along the upward path of mobility to financial security, and, indeed, many who do this amass great wealth and property. But when the wealthy one finally reaches the "rest" of his retirement, to enjoy the "goods" of his accumulation—"the reward allotted to him", due to the priorities of his life—is he oblivious to how much he has missed and how little time he has left "until he leaves them to others and dies"?

Sirach has more to say about the ambitious, and particularly the battle that rages between the classes, which still applies today, even in our modern supposedly classless society:

> Humility is an abomination to a proud man;
>   likewise a poor man is an abomination to a rich one.
> When a rich man totters, he is steadied by friends,
>   but when a humble man falls,
>   he is even pushed away by friends.
> If a rich man slips, his helpers are many;
>   he speaks unseemly words, and they justify him.
> If a humble man slips, they even reproach him;
>   he speaks sensibly, and receives no attention.
> When the rich man speaks all are silent,
>   and they extol to the clouds what he says.
> When the poor man speaks they say, "Who is this fellow?"
>   And should he stumble, they even push him down.
>   (13:20–23)

I was tempted to say this sounds a bit like today's atmosphere within the beltway of our nation's capital, but, frankly, how is this not descriptive of life in most of today's cities worldwide?

Sirach, however, describes another, simpler man, "who is slow and needs help, who lacks strength and abounds in poverty" (11:12). Just as our Lord proclaimed that the "poor in spirit" as well as "those who mourn" and "the meek" are "blessed" (Mt 5:3, 4, 5), Sirach wrote that "the eyes of the Lord look upon him for his good; he lifts him out of his low estate and raises up his head, so that many are amazed at him" (11:12–13).

It is critical to recognize that God sees through different eyes from those around us in this frantic, ambitious river. He sees our heart, our motives, our conscience, our contentment, as well as our ignorance, and in the end He evaluates our needs by the yardstick of being "good". He responds in ways that "pass all understanding", especially to those who have resisted the temptation of trusting in worldly "security" for the peace, contentment, and strength of Christ (see Phil 4:6–13).

This description of the poor man sounds like another that a great biblical prophet once described:

He had no form or comeliness that
    we should look at him,
and no beauty that we should
    desire him.
He was despised and rejected by
    men;
a man of sorrows, and acquainted
    with grief;
and as one from whom men hide
    their faces
he was despised, and we esteemed
    him not. (Is 53:2–3)

So to whom in this unruly river do we listen? Whom do we seek to follow and emulate? And whose advice do we shun? Do we mostly trust and follow the rich and successful, the confident and charismatic, the attractive and winsome? "When the rich man speaks", do we listen in silence and "extol to the clouds what he says"? And "when the poor man speaks", or one who has chosen a simpler life of less and less, do we respond, "Who is this fellow?" and "even push him down"?

Do we merely patronize the poor and the humble, the simple and less ambitious? I wonder whether we would listen to the advice of a financial analyst if he fit Isaiah's description of our Lord.

Happy Is as Happy Does

The assumption of the majority of our fellow frogs is that there are always natural causes for all of life. If we're healthy or we get cancer, it must be a function of our diet or exercise; if we get rich or end up poor, it is because we were either ambitious or lazy or because we invested well or poorly; if our life is a failure or a success, it all comes back to something we did or didn't do.

Certainly our actions affect our lives and the lives of others, as well as the world around us, but, as Sirach points out, the truth of life is far more mysterious: "Good things and bad ["prosperity and adversity", KJV], life and death, poverty and wealth, come from the Lord" (11:14).

It might be that there is far less connection than we suspect between what we eat or how we live and the good or bad events of life. It might be more a matter of God using whatever means are necessary to get our attention away from our false gods and back to Him. What is important is that we realize as soon as possible, before we are swept away by the pressure of the ambitious who are swimming beside us, that, as Mother Teresa said, it's not about being successful, but being faithful. As Sirach put it: "The gift of the Lord endures for those who are godly, and what he approves will have lasting success" (11:17).

In other words, whatever peace and security we may want for our future comes not necessarily as a direct result of our ambitious efforts but as a "gift of the Lord" to those who focus their lives on being "godly", or like Him. This involves recognizing that the things we do that meet His approval are the things that "have lasting success" and therefore lasting value.

What does this say, though, about the direction of our lives? About our commitments and investments? Sirach next makes a statement that almost makes it sound as if we should just go with the flow, not swerving from the course we have already taken, even if we are but frogs floating along in a river of progress: "Stand by your covenant and attend to it, and grow old in your work" (11:20).

What we are truly being called to do, however, is to cut through the blinding crust of our assumptions and commitments to rediscover the one true underlying covenant of our being: that we were created in love in the image of our Creator God, who established a covenant with His people, which has been fulfilled in Christ and into which we are adopted through baptism. As John wrote, "See what love the Father has given us, that we should be called children of God; and so we are" (1 Jn 3:1). Here again is that challenging purpose for which we were created: to know, love, and serve God in this life and to be happy with Him forever. It is by *this* covenant—this purpose—that we must joyfully stand and to which we must attend, not merely enduring our present work for the hope of future happiness, but rather being willing to "grow old in our work", fulfilling our purpose and seeking His face in the simplicity of the present moment.

Happy Is What Happy Trusts

The success stories and motivational PowerPoint presentations of those who are apparently succeeding on the crowded escalator of financial materialism can certainly be distracting. It can make one's heart question or second-guess any thought of turning from this highly promoted route of financial security. It seems so much easier just to get on board and blindly allow the culture to carry us along in its direction. We feel more secure being pulled along, mindlessly, our ears and minds numbed by earbuds, trusting that the confident culture around us is leading us to a better future.

Every man, though, is a sinner and can be wrong about the future. Therefore, Sirach tells us, we must "not wonder at the works of a sinner, but trust in the Lord and keep at your toil" (11:21).

Every successful investor can be wrong in the evaluations and explanations of how what he did was the key to his success—as well as yours! In reality, the blessings of the rich may have had little to do with their well-calculated human efforts and may be as fleeting as a surprise blessing can change the life of a poor man:

For it is easy in the sight of the Lord
   to enrich a poor man quickly and suddenly.
The blessing of the Lord is the reward of the godly,
   and quickly God causes his blessing to flourish.

(11:21–22)

Everything comes from God, whose priority is to "reward ... the godly", and the timing of His rewards is also according to His priorities. No one except God knows tomorrow—not even the most astute financial analyst and his carefully developed computer models of anticipated stock performance. Therefore, as Sirach warns,

Do not say, "What do I need,
   and what prosperity could be mine in the future?"
Do not say, "I have enough,
   and what calamity could happen to me in the future?"
In the day of prosperity, adversity is forgotten,
   and in the day of adversity, prosperity is not remembered.

(11:23–25)

This reminds me of hearing my banker explain, with cocky assurance, how my own investment portfolio was on track to provide all my family's future needs—one month before everything crashed in 2008! And what about those who at the same time had just decided their portfolios had reached sufficient security for them to retire— only to discover a month later that their net worth had been cut in half! John Steinbeck's superb book *The Grapes of Wrath* beautifully illustrates how "in the day of prosperity, adversity is forgotten, and in the day of adversity, prosperity is not remembered."

When the Soup Is Cooked

Returning to the imagery of frog soup, I suppose that wondering, "When is the soup cooked?" is another way of wondering, "What will be the result of the present trajectory of our lives?" Sirach makes the following statement about the end:

For it is easy in the sight of the Lord
>   to reward a man on the day of death according to his
>   conduct.
> The misery of an hour makes one forget luxury,
>   and at the close of a man's life his deeds will be revealed.
> Call no one happy before his death;
>   a man will be known through his children. (11:26–28)

How will we "be known through [our] children"? What will we have left them? Will they remember us as people who sacrificed everything to gamble on some fleeting financially secure future of things and wealth? Or as people who were willing to sacrifice everything except to love God and to love them, to enjoy being with them, to "have no anxiety about anything", not to "complain of want" but "in whatever state ... to be content" (Phil 4:6, 11), and to find ways to honor God in everything we did?

Remember that no one can read anyone else's mind; no one—even the best counselor or confessor—knows the truth of our innermost thoughts. So when we look at someone's life and determine that he must be *happy*, we may be very, very wrong, for in the end it may be only those closest to a person—and after he is gone, that will  be only his children—who truly have an inkling of whether in this life he ever experienced true happiness.

If we are willing to reconsider the present trajectory of our financial priorities, Sirach is not through hitting us in the solar plexus:

> Do not revel in great luxury,
>   lest you become impoverished by its expense.
> Do not become a beggar by feasting with borrowed money,
>   when you have nothing in your purse. (18:32–33)

Boy, ain't this descriptive of our present financial mess, especially the unfathomable trajectory of our present national debt! We have dug a bottomless pit of debt because, as a nation, we "revel in great luxury"—blessings upon blessings that we gradually have taken for granted as rights. As a nation, we have "progressed" beyond the simplicity of the responsibly contented to the upward mobility of the irresponsibly greedy, and even though our federal government has long since bypassed our budget and resources, we continue to demand the luxuries of our Americanism, which, of course, "is ours by right"! As a result, we, as a nation and as individuals, have been oblivious to advice such as "Do not become a beggar by feasting with borrowed money, when you have nothing in your purse." *Mea culpa! Mea culpa! Mea maxima culpa!*

Saint Paul warned the young novice bishop Saint Timothy that this pervasive selfish greed would be a sign of the end times:

> But understand this, that in the last days there will come times of stress. For men will be lovers of self, lovers of money, proud, arrogant, abusive, disobedient to their parents, ungrateful, unholy, inhuman, implacable, slanderers, profligates, fierce, haters of good, treacherous, reckless, swollen with conceit, lovers of pleasure rather than lovers of God, holding the form of religion but denying the power of it. Avoid such people. (2 Tim 3:1–5)

The more we can, by grace, extricate ourselves and our families from the encumbrances of this soup or river (this world) in which we live, the freer we can be to live without anxiety and for the glory of God. This does not mean that everyone must escape to the country and take up sustainable farming. However, it is undeniably more difficult to detach ourselves from the priorities and temptations of our modern culture, the more we are planted in the midst of it, struggling against the pressures  of the crowd, like the bats in our barn rafters. Yet, going into debt to set up shop in a rural setting makes no sense either. Rather, we must begin by trusting that wherever we are at this moment is precisely where God intends us to be *at this moment* and—as pointed out in an

earlier chapter with a quote from Jeremiah—where we are to seek
His welfare. It is here that we are called to live gospel simplicity:

> Do not love the world or the things in the world. If any one loves the
> world, love for the Father is not in him. For all that is in the world,
> the lust of the flesh and the lust of the eyes and the pride of life, is
> not of the Father but is of the world. And the world passes away,
> and the lust of it; but he who does the will of God abides for ever.
> (1 Jn 2:15–17)

Or, as the author of Hebrews warned, "Keep your life free from love
of money, and be content with what you have; for he has said, 'I will
never fail you nor forsake you'" (13:5).

Along the same lines, seventeenth-century French theologian and
bishop Jacques-Bénigne Bossuet urged:

> Let us join St. Philip in saying with all our heart, "Lord, show us the
> Father, and we shall be satisfied." He alone can fill all our emptiness,
> satisfy all our needs, content us, and make us happy. Let us then empty
> our hearts of all other things, for if the Father alone suffices, then we
> have no need for sensible goods, less for exterior wealth, and still less
> for the honor of men's good opinion....
>
> To own things as though one had nothing, to be married as though
> one were not, to make use of this world as though one were not using
> it, but as though it did not exist, and as though we were not a part
> of it: this is the true good for which we should strive.[2]

In this, Bossuet was merely reiterating what Saint Augustine had
said centuries before: "[The Christian] ought to use the world, not
become its slave. [This] means having, as though not having."[3] A
final word from Father Thomas Dubay, God rest his soul: "Poverty
of fact and of spirit contributes to the radical self-emptying that is a
condition for this fullness of prayer and joy: 'Having nothing, pos-
sessing all things' (2 Cor 6:10). God forces himself on no one. If I

[2] Jacques-Bénigne Bossuet, *Meditations for Lent*, ed. and trans. Christopher O. Blum (Man-
chester, N.H.: Sophia Institute Press, 2013), 10–11.
[3] Saint Augustine, Discourse on Psalm 95.

cling to things, he lets me have my things. If I am empty of things, he fills me with himself."[4]

As I've admitted several times in this book, I myself have a long way to grow, as I struggle in the current of this present economic river. May the Lord help us empty ourselves of anything that keeps us from swimming in His direction.

[4] Thomas Dubay, *Happy Are You Poor* (San Francisco: Ignatius Press, 1981), 164.

The Rural Life

*There is great gain in godliness with contentment; for we
brought nothing into the world, and we cannot take anything
out of the world; but if we have food and clothing, with these we
shall be content.*

*But those who desire to be rich fall into temptation, into a
snare, into many senseless and hurtful desires that plunge men
into ruin and destruction. For the love of money is the root of all
evils; it is through this craving that some have wandered away
from the faith and pierced their hearts with many pangs.*

—1 Timothy 6:6–10

Whether our neighbors, coworkers, financial advisers, or
all the pundits on the evening
news call it this, we are all by
design striving for the "good
life" or, better termed, happiness. God created us to seek this
and (to succumb to a modern
image) programmed this into
our souls to draw us toward Him (as expressed by both Saint Augus-
tine and Blaise Pascal). The voices in the swift flowing cultural river
around us, however, might distract us from this ultimate and blessed
quest—coaxing and drawing us along toward a supposed good life
that might not be so good after all.

So what is the good life? How does one attain it? Let me begin
with a disclaimer: there are far sharper knives in the drawer than I for
this task, but given my butter-knife mentality, let me take a stab at

pointing out why I have come to believe that the rural life may be the place most conducive to attaining the good life, particularly for souls as weak in self-discipline as I. Most of us, I believe, fail to experience the good life because we float around too blindly in this soup of convenience, complacency, and imitation goodness.

My family and I certainly love our rural life on this land. (Admittedly, we didn't arrive here as the result of great wisdom, but more as the result of inheritance. And it ain't all a bed of roses; from my back porch, I can easily identify dozens of tasks yet to be started that need to be completed before winter sets in.) But just because it's nice out here and potentially less cluttered by distracting voices doesn't mean that one cannot attain the good life in the city.

So how does one aim at attaining the good life? Is there any valid argument that the best place to seek and find the good life is in a rural setting? Or, maybe to state it even more boldly: *Why farm?*

What I will share in this chapter is gleaned from a book whose title confidently proclaims, *The Importance of the Rural Life, According to the Philosophy of St. Thomas Aquinas*. This "study in economic philosophy" was the doctoral dissertation of George H. Speltz, a priest of the Diocese of Winona, and was originally published in 1944. Fr. Speltz eventually became a rural bishop and served as president of the National Catholic Rural Life Conference. Possibly, as with Monsignor Ligutti's book, the distractions of the Second World War caused this book's insights to rest unnoticed as it gathered dust on seldom-perused library shelves until it was recently reissued.

This book is well worth reading carefully from beginning to end, but the following are selective quotes from Bishop Speltz's summary of Thomas Aquinas' argument in favor of the rural life and the dignified life and exalted work of the husbandman (i.e., the farmer):

> According to the Angelic Doctor the "good life" involves other values besides the spiritual.... Man, he affirms, is composed of body as well as of soul. Accordingly, anything that helps to conserve the life of man represents a good for him.... Even though [man] be virtuous he can yet suffer evil through the lack of bodily goods; and having fallen into this evil he will be sorrowful.[1]

---

[1] George H. Speltz, *The Importance of the Rural Life, According to the Philosophy of St. Thomas Aquinas* (1944; reissue, Lexington: St. Pius X Press, 2011), 2.

Most people today think of the good life as attaining the pinnacle of good health and prosperity. Passing recently through an airport terminal, I dodged into a kiosk for a book or magazine. There before me was a new magazine entitled, of all things, *The Good Life*. A quick glance confirmed my suspicions: good health, fitness, and affluence. Is this all or primarily what the good life means?

Even many modern Christian sects proclaim that the good life promised by Jesus Christ is one of health and wealth. They accumulate Scripture passages that when combined seem to suggest that the blessings that God promises the faithful are all earthly blessings. They tend to ignore verses in which Christ warns, "Take heed, and beware of all covetousness; for a man's life does not consist in the abundance of his possessions" (Lk 12:15).

On the other hand, other modern Christians take the opposite approach. Like modern Stoics or Gnostics, they emphasize only the soul, almost to the detriment of the body. The true good life (happiness), however, is a betterment not only of the soul but of the body and the soul, the whole person. Consequently, it is essential to recognize that it is difficult to have a happy soul (to grow in holiness) if the needs of the body are not met.

> An adequate provision of material goods is necessary for the practice of virtue. [Consequently] St. Thomas does not regard it as unbecoming for man to work with the material goods of this earth in order that they may serve the purpose for which they were created—human needs—as perfectly as possible.[2]

Spending many hours each day getting our hands dirty until our muscles ache is a good thing, as long as the end, or goal, of our work is good.

> St. Thomas insures against an overemphasis of bodily goods by calling them "Instrumental." ... In practice, however, modern man has become inordinately preoccupied with them.[3]

All material goods in this world are instrumental means to the ends for which they were created. Material goods are not ends in themselves.

[2] Ibid., 3–4.
[3] Ibid., 4.

In our sinfulness, however, we "become inordinately preoccupied with them" as ends that we dedicate our time, talents, and money to accumulate, even to hoard.

> The Thomistic synthesis provides against this disorder by pegging material goods into a fixed place within the hierarchy of man's need. This is achieved in part, by relegating them as means to an end that is outside and above them, to an end that is fixed and capable of controlling them. . . .
> [Material] goods that pertain to the conservation of an individual, i.e., those that are immediately ordered to a fundamental need of the body, as food and drink, are called goods of the body (*bonum corporis*); those that are not ordered in a general way to human needs, fall into the class of external goods (*bonum exterius*). Such are riches (*divitiae*). Of these two classes of material goods, those called "bodily goods" are the higher because necessary for the practice of virtue.[4]

Not all material goods are equal instruments because the ends for which they were created are not equal: the highest goods, of course, are those that unite us with God (divine goods); the second highest are those that nurture our soul; the third highest are bodily goods, which provide the needs of the body (food, drink, clothing, shelter) and enable us to reach for the higher goods; and the lowest are the rest, external goods: they do not naturally unite us with God, nurture our soul, or provide for our bodily needs. This is one of the many mistakes of the modern "health and wealth" preachers. They don't merely promise the necessary bodily goods but point to the acquisition and accumulation of external lesser goods as the sure sign of God's blessing. Certainly God can use anything by grace to bring us to Him, but this is out of the ordinary. We must beware of using this as an excuse for accumulating these lesser material goods.

> The amount of [bodily goods] necessary for the practice of virtue, and consequently for the good life, is strictly limited, a truth emphasized both by Aristotle and by Aquinas. On the other hand, external goods, namely riches, inasmuch as they are ordered only in a general manner to human needs, are not regarded as essential for "an act of virtue."

[4] Ibid., 5.

Since riches are sought for their power to procure other things rather than for the direct satisfaction of some bodily need, they easily come to be desired inordinately.... As a result of this inordinate desire for riches man is unduly preoccupied with the quest for material goods, failing to realize, as St. Thomas points out, that riches are the least among human goods.[5]

Bodily goods are self-regulating, whereas exterior goods are not: normally we can eat only so much, drink only so much, wear only so many clothes, and need only so much shelter. A person can determine how much he needs to eat or drink in a day, a week, a month, and a year and plan, procure, and store this. A person can also determine what kinds of clothes he needs to meet the demands of the climate in which he lives and plan, procure, and store this. And a person can determine how much he needs to shelter himself and his family and then build and maintain it. Certainly, our concupiscence can lead us to crave more food, drink, clothing, and shelter than we need, like the man in the Gospel who tore down his old barns to build new ones, but still, we always can compare what we have, or want to have, to what we really need.

With the lesser exterior goods, essentially anything at all is over and above what we need. Certainly God has created and allowed these external goods for our enjoyment. Our concupiscence, though, can convince us that we need these things—to keep up with the Joneses, or to sustain our reputation in the community or in our state of life, or just because we have more than enough money to provide for our bodily needs. With no obvious need level, there is no limit to the amount of material goods we can justify for ourselves, and we can become so attached to them that we become convinced we cannot live without them.

Guided by this scale of values, St. Thomas gives an eminent place in the hierarchy of human activities to the life of the husbandman [i.e., farmer], whose work is ordered to the procuring of bodily goods for the immediate use of the household.... As a corollary of their teaching on the secondary place of external goods, both Aristotle and Aquinas warned against the practice of trading. Because of the latent

[5] Ibid., 5–6.

greed in men, those who traded might easily fall into the practice of trading for the purpose merely of amassing external goods. Such trading would be directed to the unnatural and limitless end of amassing money, ever more money.[6]

Contrary to our modern culture's view, Aquinas ranked the husbandman as having one of the highest occupations in the community of man, comparable to a teacher or a doctor (and possibly at the other end of the scale from politicians; as G. K. Chesterton would later quip, "It is terrible to contemplate how few politicians are hanged"[7]). Aquinas considered the work of the husbandman "noble in its purpose, namely, to provide the necessities of life",[8] which are needed for the nourishment of the soul, leading to union with God. Most other occupations focus on producing, trading, or selling external goods that fulfill no inherent eternal need and serve no purpose. This does not mean that these lesser things or these occupations are evil, for the technology to produce them are gifts of God's creation. However, as lesser goods with no inherent limitation, they can be desired inordinately.

> Since the need of any one household for natural wealth, such as food and clothing, is limited, so also the activity of the husbandman, as long as it was directed to the procuring of the bodily goods and not of external goods primarily, was proportionately limited and tended less to become inordinate. It was comparatively easy in the agrarian way of life advocated by Aristotle and Aquinas, for the people to retain a true evaluation of bodily goods, as opposed to external goods, the former having a fixed relation to the needs of the various households.[9]

In other words, when most families lived in a rural setting, in small communities in which generally everyone was content with producing sufficient bodily goods, a farmer's work and life were also, therefore, limited. Though farm work was hard and physically demanding, the farmer knew when his work was done. He could relax contented once he had done all that was necessary that day to provide for the

[6] Ibid.
[7] G. K. Chesterton, interview, *Cleveland Press*, March 1, 1921.
[8] Speltz, *The Importance of the Rural Life*, 16.
[9] Ibid., 6.

bodily needs of his family. As long as they lived untouched by the obsession of the outside world for lesser material goods, the simple contented farm family lived happily, content with their food, drink, clothing, shelter, and the spiritual enrichment of their local parish.

However, when the simplicity of the rural farm family was shattered by the lure of the city, when farm children were lured away to work in factories, or to train in colleges for leadership roles in factories, trading houses, or investment firms, not for the procurement of more bodily goods or spiritual enrichment but "for wealth and what it will buy",[10] their lives became limitlessly driven. Or, as the post–World War I song taunted, "How Ya Gonna Keep 'Em Down on the Farm, After They've Seen Paree?"[11]

Even the natural limits of bodily goods became shattered. Today, when does one ever have enough specialty foods, flavored cappuccinos, designer clothing, and suburban sprawl homes, not to mention electronics, cars, toys, books, CDs, DVDs, games, and money? When can anyone sit back and relax, content that he has produced and accumulated all the bodily and material goods he will ever need? When have we reached our "number" to know we have invested enough in our 401(k)s to provide all the goods we will need to keep us in the lifestyle to which we have become accustomed until we die—with our life expectancy today being extended longer and longer!

And one last thing, though Bishop Speltz and Thomas Aquinas have much, much more to say!

> The husbandman uses his rational faculties to direct the organic and non-organic forces of nature to the production of new things.... The agricultural worker is distinguished from his fellow manual laborers in this, that it is given to him to participate in this cooperation with God in a unique way.... The non-agricultural worker, on the other hand, even though he does impart greater utility and beauty to the things of earth, yet he cannot really be said to be making the earth bring forth new basic materials. This is the task of the husbandman. When he acts as an instrumental cause in God's hands, he releases

---

[10] Hank Williams Sr., "House of Gold", Sony/ATV Music Publishing LLC, Warner/Chappell Music.

[11] Lyrics by Joe Young and Sam M. Lewis; music by Walter Donaldson (New York: Waterson, Berlin and Snyder, 1919).

a host of natural, organic causes. He taps the fonts of productivity which God has placed in things.... The art of husbandry, which produces the fruits of the earth in cooperation with an interior principle of nature, namely, its organic powers, therefore shares in some way the dignity of the arts of teaching and medicine, and exceeds in dignity the art of carpentry.[12]

The farmer uniquely taps directly into the creative energies that God instilled into His creation to provide for the bodily goods of his family, his community, and the world. When he grows vegetables or raises cattle, he is cooperating with God's creative grace. The farmer is not doing anything but helping God's creation provide the food, drink, clothing, and shelter that God had already empowered His creation to produce.

All technologies that underlie all other occupations at their core emerge from the gifts that God planted in His creation and, to varying degrees, especially guided by grace, can lead to the production and nurturing of the higher goods. However, because they can be so readily used to produce the lesser external goods, the ever tempting voices of "the world, the flesh, and the devil" can drive the use of these technologies and their related occupations to such an inordinate extent that reason can no longer limit their use.

For example, the technology to build a computer chip is a gift of God, and the benefits from this technology have so altered our lives that it is close to impossible to envision life without it. There are many ways in which this technology has been used to provide the higher goods of bringing people closer to God, enriching their souls, and providing for their bodily needs. Yet we all know to what pervasive extent this technology has also been used to fill our world with lesser goods—with gadgets we really don't need yet have grown as a culture to believe we do need and cannot live without—and that any efforts to produce, advance, and extend these technologies are justified. But does the good of smartphones for the affluent in first-world nations justify the inordinate use of third-world factory workers in a sweatshop? These poor third-world workers are not producing anything that meets their own bodily needs, nor is their

---

[12] Speltz, *The Importance of the Rural Life*, 17, 53–55.

work in any way naturally limited: they will work as long as their employer demands—as many hours and days as he demands, to produce as many products as he deems necessary to produce the money he believes he needs—so they can scratch out enough money, they hope, to provide for the bodily needs of their families.

The problem is that we live in a culture that places its highest value on the production of and lust for the lesser material goods; even the "poor" are defined not by their lack of goods to meet their bodily needs but by their inability to procure the lesser material goods that our culture considers their rights in our civilized state. Far too many people on welfare, labeled poor by our government, have cell phones, HDTVs, cable, air-conditioning, and more than one car per family and, per government reports, are not starving but are generally overweight. (This last point is complicated because too often the only food and drink available to the poor is less than beneficial and full of trans fats, sugar, et cetera, whereas healthful food, such as fresh produce, is either too expensive or, for those living in the inner city, often simply inaccessible.)

Ironically, our culture has become obsessed with providing insured health care for every single person, so that everyone can live as long as possible. Is this so that everyone can have more time to grow in holiness and eventual union with God? Or even to enjoy as long as possible a simple life contented with their basic needs? No, it is so they can enjoy and have more and more of the lesser external goods, which have no natural limits, in full-service condominium communities with full-time nursing services, near golf courses with paved pathways for their Medicare-financed Hoverounds. Lord, help us.

We live in a culture, an entire world, that has it all backward—that rewards and honors those who dedicate their entire lives to producing, promoting, and getting rich on the lesser material goods of this world, all of which remain in the box when the lid is closed on this life.[13] Yet this culture of ours also looks askance at, even denigrates, those who have chosen a simpler rural life, who have dedicated their lives to providing for their families those things—and maybe only those things—that are most essential. Just think how our culture—how we ourselves—too often looks down on families

[13] I talk more about this in chapter 15, "Salvation Is Nearer Than You Think".

who have little more than enough material goods to provide for their bodily needs, yet their existence is far more in line with that promoted and lived by our Lord Jesus, His disciples, Francis of Assisi, and other holy Christians throughout the ages.

The problem is that these values of our culture have so infiltrated every aspect of our lives that an increasing number of those dedicated to providing for the basic bodily needs of our world—food, clothing, shelter, and even spiritual enrichment—are encouraged to do so primarily to accumulate more and more money—not to provide the top three levels of goodness, but to fill their lives with lesser material things. Agribusinessmen, as modern farmers prefer to be called, now use hundreds of thousands of dollars' worth of high-tech equipment to farm thousands of acres to provide high-yield hybrid and genetically modified crops. They do this to make sufficient profit to provide not only the food, drink, clothing, and shelter their families need, but also the external goods they deem necessary to consider themselves as progressive as the city dwellers they see portrayed on network television.

So, if any of this is true, what does it say to most of us who not only have chosen to focus our time, talent, and energies on occupations other than husbandry and to live in nonrural settings but also believe that God has called us to do so? Regardless of where we live or what we must do to provide sustenance for ourselves and our families, here are a few suggestions as to where we might begin:

- Pray for forgiveness for all the ways in which our lives have been driven by "want of wealth and what it can buy".
- Meditate daily on the New Testament teachings on gospel simplicity. Pray for clarity and guidance as to how the Lord wants us to live this out in our particular circumstances.
- Look more closely at our stuff and recognize how much of it consists of lesser, nonessential goods. Consider how much of our lives have become subsumed in accumulating and hoarding these nonessentials.
- Every time we believe we must go shopping, consider whether what we are tempted to buy is necessary for the bodily needs of our family or merely another unnecessary, lesser material entanglement that one day we may wish we had never bought in the first place.

- Pray for the freeing grace of detachment. How many things do we own that if taken away would truly devastate us? Ask God to give us the grace to start letting go of things, even giving them away to friends, family, and especially agencies that serve the needy.
- Recognize that, even if we believe that our present accumulation of stuff is not harmful to our spiritual life, it might be setting an unsustainable example for our children and grandchildren. By grace, we might have become sufficiently detached from our stuff; we might have convinced ourselves that if we lost it all tomorrow, we would be just fine. We might have quit buying more and more and have become content with living more simply. Then the question arises whether it is necessary to continue divesting ourselves of the remaining stuff that surrounds us. "I just might need that widget tomorrow, and if it's gone, I might regret it!" How much more loudly does our accumulation speak than the convictions of our heart? Does our remaining accumulation present a continuing contradiction to our well-meaning words? Our conflicting examples might be setting up our children and grandchildren for a life of even more escalating accumulation, because the cultural river in which our children swim tells them that success is measured by how much more stuff they attain than their parents.

Allow me to add a personal illustration. The elderly mother of a very close friend (names withheld to protect the innocent) died recently. She had always been a discerning collector of books, audio and video recordings, teddy bears, figurines, pottery, and dolls. Especially during the ten years after her husband died, and as she became less mobile, she increasingly surrounded herself with the stuff that brought her joy. Maybe it was because she had been born immediately after the 1929 stock market crash and had lived through the poverty of the Depression and then WW II that she encamped within the security of things.

It wasn't until after her passing, when her children began taking inventory of the estate, that they became fully aware of the extent to which she had evolved from a collector into an addicted hoarder. Closets and cupboards, shelves and display cabinets were overflowing with thousands of records, cassette tapes, VHS tapes, and CDs. At an average of ten dollars per item, the original cost must have topped twenty-five thousand dollars! When purchased, these recordings may have held some investment value, but with the accelerating *progress* of today's digital age of instant accessibility and gratification, this physical cache of recordings has become essentially worthless. And the collections of bears, dolls, figurines, bottles, porcelain houses, and pottery, also originally worth thousands of dollars, are of little redeemable value, except to serious collectors or perhaps other addicted hoarders.

Now the family is stuck wondering what to do with all this stuff. They had already become convicted about living simpler lives, trying to detach themselves from our culture's constant pressure to buy and hoard more and more, but now they have inherited a second house, which because of nostalgia will be hard to sell and which is overflowing with essentially worthless stuff that also will be difficult to sell. And because they have become convinced of the necessity of living more simply, they are hesitant to burden someone else with this stuff, even by just giving it away. They could bag it all up and throw it away, but is this being a good steward of the dreams of their mother, who bought this stuff thinking it would be of some value to pass on to her children? She wanted to bless their lives; she had no idea to what extent her collections had become a curse.

When we die, and our closets, shelves, cupboards, display cabinets, garages, and storage units (or barns) are opened for inventory, what will our "collecting" tell our children about our commitment to living Christ-centered, simpler lives?

Allow me to add one more caveat, maybe a bit controversial, but I believe potentially critical to the future of our children and grandchildren. In *The Unsettling of America*, Wendell Berry wrote:

> [Bernard DeVoto, in *The Course of Empire* wrote]: "The first belt-knife given by a European to an Indian was a portent as great as the cloud that mushroomed over Hiroshima.... Instantly the man of 6000 B.C. was bound fast to a way of life that had developed seven and a half millennia beyond his own. He began to live better and began to die." The principal European trade goods were tools, cloth, weapons, ornaments, novelties, and alcohol. The sudden availability of these things produced a revolution that affected every aspect of Indian life.[14]

[14] Wendell Berry, *The Unsettling of America* (San Francisco: Sierra Club Books, 1996), 5, quoting Bernard DeVoto, *The Course of Empire* (Boston: Houghton Mifflin, 1952), 92–93.

In other words, the European imperialists tempted the Native Americans, through the gifts of lesser, nonessential goods, to give up their land, their rights, their livelihood, and eventually their lives. Berry used this analogy to show how modern industrialism has tempted farmers to give up their settled rural lives for the unsettled progressiveness of the cities. But this analogy reminds me of something that is even more potentially dangerous for our children, for it sounds amazingly similar to how China, or international investors using Chinese or other Asian workers, has been wooing American citizens through the myriad of local and online "outlet stores" with cheap, lesser, nonessential trinkets. What is even more shocking, from the perspective of our free-world, democratic, capitalistic assumptions, is that the International Monetary Fund now reports that Communist China has overtaken the United States as the world's largest economy![15] As I write this, a news headline reads: "Pentagon Fears Chinese Military Advances Will Overtake USA's in Five Years". Lord, help us. Also as I write, Russia has just invaded a neighboring sovereign nation and annexed Crimea. Yet the European nations and the United States are showing no willingness to stand up against this abuse of power—not so much for fear of war, but for fear of jeopardizing their economies and access to the resources that power the technologies that now control their lives. Even more frightening, though, the same radical Islamic hordes that threatened to destroy Western civilization in the Middle Ages are today on the rise, marching through the Middle East, turning their captured territories into a new independent Islamic state, willing to behead anyone in their path who does not agree with them—or die in the process.

Consider to what extent we can spend the remainder of our lives divesting ourselves of unnecessary things beyond our bodily needs, to live more and more simply, whether we live in a rural setting or a high-rise apartment in downtown Manhattan. I believe this is the best thing we can do for our children, our grandchildren, and ourselves. Then, through the assistance of grace, we may be able to live out what our Lord and His disciples taught us:

[15] Mike Bird, "China Just Overtook the US as the World's Largest Economy", *Business Insider Singapore*, October 8, 2014, http://www.businessinsider.sg/china-overtakes-us-as-worlds-largest-economy-2014-10/#.VIHRS9athVc.

Sell your possessions, and give alms; provide yourselves with purses that do not grow old, with a treasure in the heavens that does not fail, where no thief approaches and no moth destroys. (Lk 12:33)

Do not lay up for yourselves treasures on earth, where moth and rust consume and where thieves break in and steal, but lay up for yourselves treasures in heaven, where neither moth nor rust consumes and where thieves do not break in and steal. For where your treasure is, there will your heart be also. (Mt 6:19–21)

I'm hesitant to do this—because I recognize that I am not a qualified financial adviser—but what Thomas Aquinas said, as summarized by Bishop Speltz, seems to establish a workable guideline for what we must do to plan for our economic futures. That banker I mentioned earlier had asked me what I thought my wife and I would need annually to support ourselves after I "retire" (whatever that is). Fifty thousand dollars? A hundred thousand? A gazillion? I had no clue how to respond because (without my having done any of the reflections mentioned in this book) our life had become so full of unnecessary stuff and the maintenance of it and the presumed goal of accumulating more.

Using the advice of Aquinas and Bishop Speltz, however, provides a much more workable approach. Let me begin by emphasizing that the question "What will you or your family need for the future?" is not the right question, for it blindly presumes the individualism of our modern culture. It is not merely what I, or my wife and I, or my family and I will need, but what we will need within the community in which we live, or need to live. In the same way that the salvation of our souls was never intended to be an individualistic matter but rather a matter of living as faithful individuals within the community or People of God,[16] so we were created to live within extended communities, in which we help provide for each other's needs. This is the core of subsidiarity: what we cannot provide for ourselves, our immediate community can and should provide. Therefore, it's not merely about providing enough investments in stocks and bonds on the chance that the eventual profits will provide enough capital

---

[16] See my book *What Must I Do to Be Saved?* (Zanesville, Ohio: Coming Home Resources, 2012).

for our individual needs; rather, we must look to the community in which we have chosen to live out the rest of our lives as the source for our shared needs.

The first and most essential things for which we will need to plan are those things that provide for our bodily needs: air, food, water, clothing, shelter, and spiritual nourishment. Air was taken for granted in Aquinas' day but not so in ours. Some of us live in polluted environments that, for our health and that of our children, we may need to leave. And spiritual nourishment, through both private devotions and the gathered local community of the Church and her sacraments, is not a mere add-on but is as essential to our well-being as are bodily goods. To deny this is to blindly starve ourselves into oblivion.

So, making a checklist, how will you and your community provide these bodily goods? Can you grow all or most of your food, or will you need to buy it? Do you have a natural source of water, or will you need to buy water from the community? Do you have sufficient clothing to last you until you die, or will you need to replenish your wardrobe? Are you mortgaged to the hilt, renting, or do you own your home outright? Can you heat your home with wood from your land, or will you need to pay for fuel or utilities? Can you walk to church, or will you need assistance in getting there?

These are the key questions for discerning your future needs. Many people spend their twilight years with only these things by necessity: confined to bed due to disability, receiving oxygen artificially, receiving food and fluids intravenously, wearing adequate clothing, having minimal but sufficient shelter, and being visited by a minister or priest. Others, however, accept this simplicity by choice: a simple home, basic but modest clothing, a garden and a full pantry, a well or a cistern, and an easy walk to church. In either case, though, with but these minimal bodily goods, a person can live for many years—and with the right heart can live in contentment.

Yet, once these basic bodily goods have been provided, there are other secondary yet necessary goods, for what are we to do with ourselves once the cupboards, refrigerator, cistern, and closets in our simple home are full? Herein lie our vocations: what we are to do with the gifts, talents, and opportunities God has provided in the unique places in which He has "exiled" us. These secondary yet essential goods are:

- work
- service
- leisure

This surely needs a much longer and more philosophical discussion, but to put it simply, we each were created to share in God's work. For the underlying goal of fulfilling our created purpose, He called us to use our time and talents productively for ends that are good, true, and beautiful. This requires prayerful discernment, as well as guidance from those we trust within our religious community. To follow Aquinas' advice, however, working to provide directly for the bodily needs of our family—the work of a husbandman—is a good and holy vocation. To what extent can we dedicate our working days to providing bodily goods for our families? What we can't grow or make, we will need to buy. To the extent that the vocation to which we are called prevents us from growing or making, we will need to provide more money to buy, preferably supporting those in our local community. This was the key to the success of the traditional, self-sustaining communities that built our nation and our world, in which each person had a working place within the community. No one starved; no one was naked or homeless; no one was unemployed if he desired to work.

But we have lost this self-sustaining world—except in small pockets, such as the Amish communities. Most of us have long since abandoned the agrarian world, following careers that not only make it hard to find time to garden or remodel our homes but have also prevented us from learning these skills or developing the necessary muscles.

Yet, if we look to a simpler future for ourselves and our families, it becomes more feasible to reconsider how we will focus our work as we grow older. If we are intent on living in the lifestyle to which we have become accustomed, overflowing with unnecessary things that have no natural limit, and especially with those addictive technologies that always require more and more costly energy, updates, syncing, et cetera, then we will have no choice except to work more and more hours and sink more and more money into investments run by people we will never see and whose values we will never know. On the other hand, the more we can shift our work to providing these bodily goods directly, through gardening or even farming on our own unmortgaged land, and developing interdependent relationships with our neighbors, the less our futures will be affected by the whims of our culture.

Next to work, service is the greatest task to which we can devote our time and talents. Once we have provided for the needs of spouse and family, how can we reach out to help those, especially the less fortunate, around us? So many thousands of people retire only to focus on themselves and on their leisure, some spending years in front of the television set watching reruns of *The Golden Girls*. It would take only a little effort, however, to find ways to give of ourselves as volunteers, and in doing so, we might find that through the joy that comes from giving, we want little beyond our basic bodily goods to find happiness.

And once our work and service are done for the day, leisure is a good gift of God's overflowing joy. This can include reading, exercise, music, games, and, yes, even television, but especially hobbies. Hobbies are a great way to experience the creative energy of God and can bring contentment and gratitude that can change an otherwise discouraged, lonely life into one of joyful giving and camaraderie.

As we make our lists in planning for the future, beyond these bodily and secondary necessary goods, we must also consider:

- transportation
- communication

When people lived in smaller, self-sufficient communities, transportation and communication were less significant issues. People could procure most of what they needed on foot or horseback and could yell across the pasture or ride to a neighbor's home for conversation. But advances in transportation and communication technologies have so reshaped our world (as illustrated with graphs in an earlier chapter) and transformed our lives and communities that it has become next to impossible for most of us to live without cars, cell phones, e-mail, the Internet, and even social networking. As we plan for the future, we need to discern how essential these technologies will be for our lives, for each will require more and more outflow of money to power, upgrade, and repair. The more we can simplify our lives, enhancing and developing the sustaining benefits of our local communities, the simpler will be the demands on our future resources and plans.

There is another obvious important issue I've left out of this list:

- health care

Should this be included in the first category as an essential bodily need? A right that every individual has for the well-being of his whole person and therefore the well-being of his soul? Of all the issues, this has become the most complicated as well as political. How much health care do we *need*? What criteria do we use to determine how much health care is necessary? The rise of the healthcare industry has exactly paralleled the rise of the industrial revolution. Driven by the altruistic goals of alleviating all suffering and pain, as well as extending life at whatever cost, coupled with the limitless potential of greed in our free-market culture, healthcare has risen, in the minds of Americans, to the top of the list of essential bodily goods. Given the fact that none of the leaders of our country or our government, or the leaders of our churches, can agree on the best approach to providing fair and adequate health care, I won't presume to know the answer. It seems to me, however, that the answer needs to be a personal one: the more we expect the government to take care of us, the less free we are to be faithful to God and to follow His radical call to detachment.

I also believe that this requires a rethinking of the place of suffering in our lives. The escalation of modern health care is built on the presumption that it is always good to alleviate pain and suffering and to extend life as long as possible. The practical spiritual discipline of voluntary fasting, on the other hand, has long been recommended to prepare us—body and soul, intellect and will—to face larger trials, through a period of lesser deprivations. Is it not possible that the lesser sufferings we experience during most of our lives are given by God as preparation for facing the larger sufferings of our later years? If all we have done all our lives is run to the doctor or take pills every time our regular routines are hampered by a minor ache or pain, is it any wonder so many of us are unprepared to face the larger sufferings that come with aging? It's a personal decision, of course, but the more we can accept suffering as a regular, even positive aspect of life, the less our lives will be subject to the politics and economics of our troubled health care system. As the apostle Paul reminded his Christian audience in Rome, "[W]e are children of God, and if children, then heirs, heirs of God and fellow heirs with Christ, *provided we suffer with him* in order that we may also be glorified with him" (Rom 8:16–17, emphasis mine).

I realize this call to accept suffering is hard to stomach. This is why modern evangelists find it much easier to fill basketball arena–size worship centers by preaching a comfort-laden "health and wealth" gospel than by preaching the gospel of Christ, who said, "Deny yourself, take up your cross, and follow me" (cf. Mt 16:24). Thomas à Kempis always seems to say it best:

> Be assured of this, that you must live a dying life. And the more completely a man dies to self, the more he begins to live to God. No man is fit to understand heavenly things, unless he is resigned to bear hardships for Christ's sake. Nothing is more acceptable to God, and nothing more salutary for yourself, than to suffer gladly for Christ's sake. And if it lies in your choice, you should choose rather to suffer hardships for Christ's sake, than to be refreshed by many consolations; for thus you will more closely resemble Christ and all His Saints. For our merit and spiritual progress does not consist in enjoying such sweetness and consolation, but rather in the bearing of great burdens and troubles.[17]

Finally, two more items are essential to the list:

- paying yourself
- paying God

Some money managers emphasize the need to "pay yourself first", setting aside 10 percent or more of savings before anything else. This is certainly an admirable goal, but where should this fit into the above list? I would suggest that providing for the basic bodily needs of one's family should always come first because bodily goods enable the whole person, body and soul, to attain the good life. Setting aside savings for the future should then precede the accumulation of all lesser external goods and should serve the primary purpose of

---

[17] Thomas à Kempis, *The Imitation of Christ* (New York: Penguin Books, 1982), 88.

providing future bodily goods. Since there is no limit to the amount of external goods we may eventually want or think we need, there is no way to determine how many gazillions we might need to save.

Paying God, however, through donations to the Church or to other charities, I believe, should take precedence over anything else on the list. The example of the widow's mite (see Lk 21:1–4) sets the standard. Before we even provide for basic bodily essentials, we should learn the practice of setting aside (i.e., letting go of) even a small portion of what God has provided for us. This becomes a regular, active expression of trust in God's providence—that He knows what we and our families will need for the future. On the other hand, adopting the strategy of paying ourselves first can become a regular, active habit of trusting the future to ourselves, our accumulation, the presumed progress of our culture, the assured rebound of our economy, and the foresight of financial analysts. Beginning with small donations, as we are able to provide more for the basic needs of our families, we can increase our giving to God; and this practice has an amazing way of instilling in us that "peace of God, which passes all understanding" (Phil 4:7).

The above suggestions can be itemized to form the basis for a future fiscal plan, but it will require a willingness to trust and to share. I'm certainly not suggesting that everyone is called to reduce their investments to these minimums, but the exercise of comparing these basic minimums with how we have presently invested our money can be enlightening.

Maybe the simplest way to sum all this up is by the following four principles:

1. Love the Lord your God with all your heart, soul, mind, and strength.
2. Love your neighbor as yourself.
3. Take joy in all the gifts God has given you.
4. Grasp as little as possible.

Please pray for me, and I'll ask God to bless you as we consider together the reasons we labor and the things for which we labor and how much of this is far, far more than what we need—and too often a hindrance to the enrichment of our souls and union with God.

12

Y2K Fifteen Years Later

A prudent man sees danger and hides himself;
but the simple go on, and suffer from it.

—Proverbs 22:3

Yesterday, digging through the bottom shelf of our basement pantry, I found there, way in the back, a sealed white bucket labeled "Wheat". As Yogi Berra once quipped, it was "déjà vu all over again".

I feel a bit sheepish admitting that I was one of those concerned about the ramifications of Y2K, the coming of the year 2000. Many of you probably remember—though most of you would probably prefer to forget or deny—that there was an endless line of chatter on all levels of the media in 1999. Most of those voices were expressing great and grave concern over what might happen when the computer clocks all turned from 12/31/99 to 01/01/00. Many thought the world would come to an end—as some coined it, TEOTWAWKI ("the end of the world as we know it"). Many Christians expected the so-called Rapture and left letters hidden for their relatives who might unfortunately be "left behind". Other Christians predicted the Second Coming and began a flurry of evangelization to save as many as possible. Many Catholic Christians anticipated the fulfillment of the "warning and the miracle" from several reported Marian apparitions, and Marian conferences increased in number tenfold. Many financial analysts warned of a great recession, if not a depression, and predicted there would be worldwide chaos as economies plummeted and cultures imploded. Maybe the largest response, though, was the exodus of thousands to the hills, where they began homesteading off the grid, stockpiling food, guns, and ammunition, and trying to learn survival skills so that they and their families could become self-sufficient.

Even scientists could not agree on what might happen, all because in the early days of computer programming, to economize on limited computer memory, dates were designated using only two digits for the year rather than four. Since, up until the onset of the new millennium, the "19" had always been assumed, what lay behind the great fear of TEOTWAWKI was that no one knew for certain whether the world's computers would interpret "00" as 2000 or 1900.

I wish I could say I was not caught up in all this, but in fact 264 days from the turn of the third millennium I published the article "The Spiritual and Material Ramifications of Y2K" in a book entitled *Millennium Insurance.*[1] I even hosted a television special back in 1999 entitled *Jubilee and Y2K,* so there is no way I can claim that the onset of the year 2000 didn't affect my family's thinking and plans on our rural land, evidenced by that sealed bucket of wheat in the picture.

We didn't move out to the country because of Y2K, but it did affect our thinking once we got there. We started building our home in the woods in 1996; we moved in in 1997; we had the "revelation" in 1998 that our old barn had been erected for more than rotting; we began resurrecting the "farm" and bought the cow in 1999; and frankly, on New Year's Eve, I sat up most of the night, waiting, wondering, and praying, but mostly watching as the television newscasts vividly portrayed, one time zone after another around the world, that Y2K was a bust, and AWWWTW ("All was well with the world").

I, for one, though, still believe that most of us missed the message of Y2K. The Catholic Marianists expected a warning and a miracle, and I believe this is precisely what the Lord did with Y2K. The problem is that few have listened.

I believe that the "warning" was a call to wake up and notice how we—as individuals, families, and a culture—had become so attached

[1] Marcus C. Grodi, David Palm, Kimberly Hahn, and Rev. Joseph M. Esper, *Millennium Insurance* (San Diego: Basilica Press, 1999).

to material goods and wealth; how our entire world was potentially on the brink of economic collapse with but the simple turning of a "99" to "00". Throughout the New Testament, throughout the history of the Church, Christians have been warned to avoid becoming too attached to the things of this world, because, as Saint Paul wrote, "we brought nothing into the world, and we cannot take anything out.... [T]hose who desire to be rich fall into temptation, into a snare, into many senseless and hurtful desires that plunge men into ruin and destruction" (1 Tim 6:7–9). The "warning" of Y2K was a God-given opportunity for industrialized humanity to examine how dangerously we had become attached to and dependent on industrial materialism. It was an opportunity for us to respond appropriately, through remorse, compassion, charity, humility, and simplicity.

The "miracle"? Nothing happened. There never has been a clear explanation from the scientific world as to why nothing happened. I suspect that behind the scenes all around the globe, thousands and thousands of dollars and man-hours were invested to ensure that nothing would happen and that this last-minute frantic effort to "save" our computer infrastructure would forever go unnoticed. So we will never know. Y2K quickly became a forgotten fear, which few want to mention. Oh, and that book on *Millennium Insurance* was quickly dropped from publication.

Few of us, though, seem to have learned anything from this "warning" and "miracle". The vivid truth is that here we are fifteen years later—as individuals, families, and a culture—far, far more attached to our material world than ever before. I believe this is partially because, with Y2K, far too many people "attached" their "detachment" to an event. Many of us adopted a detached, simpler lifestyle in fearful anticipation of what might come after Y2K, but when it came and passed without a problem, our "detachment" went with it. And those who never gave a moment's notice to the concerns of Y2K, and afterward gloated over their wise foresight, are even less willing to consider detaching themselves from the abundance of the American dream. Now, as in the story "The Boy Who Cried Wolf", it's nearly impossible to get anyone to recognize the need to detach himself from industrial materialism—even though all the financial indicators today suggest that our world is far more in danger of a recession, a depression, or even a political collapse, if not a war, than we were back in 1999.

I hesitate even more to make the following references, for it will surely label me a doomsayer, but, given the present state of our national and world economies as well as our perilous political tension, the fifth chapter of the prophet Jeremiah is worth reading prayerfully. His original target was rebellious Israel, but since the Word of God is a living message with many layers of meaning and application, we benefit by recognizing the relevance of his warnings to our modern world:

> Run back and forth through the streets of Jerusalem, look and
>   take note!
> Search her squares to see if you can find a man,
> One who does justice and seeks truth; that I may pardon her.
> Though they say, "As the LORD lives," yet they swear falsely.
> O LORD, do not your eyes look for truth?
> You have struck them down, but they felt no anguish;
> You have consumed them, but they refused to take correction.
> They have made their faces harder than rock; they have refused
>   to repent.
> Then I said, "These are only the poor, they have no sense;
> For they do not know the way of the LORD, the law of their
>   God.
> I will go to the great, and will speak to them;
> For they know the way of the LORD, the law of their God."
> But they all alike had broken the yoke, they had burst the
>   bonds. (verses 1–5)

Then comes the rhetorical conclusion of the Lord:

> Shall I not punish them for these things? says the LORD;
> And shall I not avenge myself on a nation such as this? (verse 9)

And His answer:

> Behold, I am bringing upon you a nation from afar,
>   O house of Israel, says the LORD.
> It is an enduring nation; it is an ancient nation,
> *A nation whose language you do not know,*
> *   nor can you understand what they say.* (verse 15, emphasis mine)

For Israel, it was Babylon, but for America—for Western civilization— might it be Russia, China, or radical Islamic terrorists?

Regardless of whether these ancient prophecies have anything to do with our present age, still the message remains. Our Lord continues to call us to detachment and simplicity. This, however, must not be "attached" to a day or an hour or to some potential financial or political crisis; rather, the truth that any one of us could be facing our Maker this night should be warning enough to awaken us to the dire need to simplify and detach our lives.

This is precisely what I wrote in that article in 1999. It wasn't an article about fear and trembling concerning TEOTWAWKI but rather a reminder that we have been called to "abide in him, so that when he appears we may have confidence and not shrink from him in shame at his coming" (1 Jn 2:28). For this, I shared a list of suggestions for preparing spiritually for the new millennium. Now, fifteen years later, I propose that these suggestions are as important as ever.

- **Begin by recognizing the importance of the present moment.** All we can know for sure is that God has given us each this present moment. It is here and in it that we are primarily called to be holy, to be faithful to God's call in our lives.
- **Recognize that we are on a "great pilgrimage to the house of the Father".** We should all do what we can to understand better and reconcile our relationship with God our Father, through the reading of Scripture and faithful spiritual writings, through confession, through prayer, and through reaching out in love to those around us, whom the Father loves.
- **Examine your present relationship with Christ.** Take some time to reflect prayerfully on John 15:1–11, considering whether you are a faithful branch on the vine of Christ.
- **Confess your sins.** Scripture overwhelmingly warns that sin separates us from God, and mortal sin can separate us from Him forever (see 1 Jn 1:6; 5:16–17). However, Scripture also teaches: "If we confess our sins, he is faithful and just, and will forgive our sins and cleanse us from all unrighteousness" (1 Jn 1:9). Using Scripture or an examination-of-conscience guide, turn your heart in remorseful repentance to God, and if you are

Catholic, certainly seek out a priest who will lead you through a thorough general confession.

- **Find a spiritual director.** Seek out a minister, a priest, or a religious who can serve as your spiritual director.
- **Pray without ceasing.** Establish a daily routine of prayer and meditation on Scripture and spiritual readings.
- **Return to Church!** As mentioned earlier, it is essential that we try to live out our faith not as individuals but as faithful individuals within the community or People of God. Therefore, if you have been "neglecting to meet together, as is the habit of some" (Heb 10:25), return to full and active communion in the Church, "encouraging one another, and all the more as you see the Day drawing near" (ibid.).
- **Make every effort to remain in a state of grace.** It is essential that we recognize that our abiding in Christ is a day-by-day, moment-by-moment endeavor, since each of us is constantly in a spiritual battle for his soul (see Eph 6).
- **Balance your reading, as well as all media influences.** Examine the "voices" that are feeding your mind, heart, and soul, choosing and excluding wisely, recognizing that sometimes we can become numb to how these are affecting us.
- **Reach out to others.** Realize that God has placed you in the midst of a very important "mission field" in which you are to be a shining light of faith, hope, and love. And especially remember your responsibility to the poor, homeless, widows, and prisoners: "Truly, I say to you, as you did it not to one of the least of these, you did it not to me" (Mt 25:45). If the plight of the poor is bad now, imagine what it would be like if the world faced a major crisis?
- **Desire freedom from things.** Seek a higher level of detachment from the need for material things and material comfort.
- **Remember to love your enemies.** It is particularly important that during the days ahead, if crisis indeed comes, if the acts of both ignorant and evil men make your lives and mine unreasonable and intolerable, we never forget the clear instructions of Jesus: "Love your enemies, do good to those who hate you, bless those who curse you, pray for those who abuse you" (Lk 6:27–28).
- **Discern carefully the spirits.** It is also important that you be very careful in your discernment of prophecies and the messages

of visionaries. Throughout the history of the Church, men and women have claimed special messages from God or definitive interpretations of biblical prophecy—and to different degrees the Church has examined these claims. Even today, people claiming an inside scoop on God's timetable insist that the signs of the times—climate change, imminent wars, political dishonesty, disease epidemics, economic upheavals, rampant violence and immorality—all indicate that God's just retribution is near! Well, this could be. Who are any of us to claim we know otherwise, for all Christians do profess that "He will come again to judge the living and the dead." However, the most highly respected spiritual writers, such as Saint John of the Cross, have always cautioned against basing our lives and faith on these sensual forms of personal revelation—yet never to the point of dismissing the true message of these signs of the times. We are always to watch and be ready, to live every day as if it might be our last.

- **Fast regularly.** When Jesus gave His instructions on prayer, fasting, and almsgiving, He presumed that His disciples already understood that He expected them to do these things regularly. Jesus said, "*When* you give alms ... *when* you pray ... *when* you fast" (Mt 6:2–18, emphasis mine).
- **Abide in God's Word.** Finally, along with making sure you know important prayers, complete your mental arsenal by memorizing helpful and encouraging texts of Scripture.

Looking at that sealed white bucket of wheat, now more than fifteen years later, I realize how poorly I have followed my own advice, for He will indeed come again in our lifetime: either in the clouds with the trumpets blaring, surrounded by angels ready to initiate the end of this world and the beginning of the next, or at the moment we die. And I swear, as I sat holding my mother's hand as she passed on several months ago, the final look in her eyes made it seem as if she was indeed hearing the welcoming sound of those trumpets.

So our Lord lovingly reminds us, "Therefore you also must be ready; for the Son of man is coming at an hour you do not expect" (Mt 24:44). It is not too late; there is no greater time to start getting ready than the present moment.

13

Being and Abiding

*Abide in me, and I in you. As the branch cannot bear
fruit by itself, unless it abides in the vine, neither can
you, unless you abide in me.*

—John 15:4

One of the many things I've learned from life on this land, besides how ignorant I am of farming, is that *being* on a farm is a whole lot different from *abiding* on a farm. This might seem obvious to some, but I think it's an important distinction to make.

Have you ever driven through the country, passing well-manicured farms, peaceful, docile sheep moving almost as if choreographed across the hillsides, parallel rows of corn or undulating waves of wheat or grass, or a pair of swans and their cygnets cutting across the glassy surface of a picturesque pond, and thought, "Wouldn't it be wonderful to live on that farm! What a peaceful, carefree life of detachment!"

If you were actually to buy a farm, with the fields, barns, pond, and critters, let alone a house for you and your family to live in and maintain, that would entail *being* on that farm. But then the *abiding* begins—the living on it, the *continuing, remaining* on it—and you would find that you had bought far more than a hobby: you had bought a lifestyle and a to-do list longer than a lifetime.

Being and *abiding* are two essential but different aspects of living on a farm, and for this reflection, *being* on a farm means more than a visit but begins when the family purchases a farm. At that moment, there begins a symbiotic relationship between the family and all aspects of the farm, including the seasons, the neighbors, and the wild creatures that fly over or crawl through the farm or prowl the perimeter. In one day, a family and a farm can begin *being* together, but then *abiding* together begins, which requires a long list of vanishing, or at least suppressed, vices, as well as maturing virtues, particularly perseverance, long-suffering, forgiveness, repentance, and manure spreaders full of patience.

Early one evening, as I was moving a temporary electric fence to form a new paddock into which our half-dozen hungry cattle were eager to move, I was reflecting on the recent death of a friend. As we all grow older, it's just a fact of life that more and more of our acquaintances pass on into eternity (and we're soon to join them). As I walked, now more slowly, across the pasture, I wondered about where my departed friend was among the possibilities of eternity.

The mostly high-tensile electric fence on and around our land is held up by different kinds of posts, accumulated over the years: rustic Osage orange or locust logs, treated wood, steel T, step-in poly, and fiberglass posts, plus (I'm ashamed to admit) a few living trees that were commandeered in a pinch. As I stomped into place a few fiberglass posts, I thought that all of my friends, family, and acquaintances could basically be segregated into four groups:

1. Those who have never known or believed in a Creator God and are members of no church.
2. Those who have been baptized, catechized, and gone through all the other ritual hoops but now demonstrate no active understanding of, interest in, or serious commitment to the faith. They may attend church regularly but do so more out of duty or habit, or they have drifted away from any active involvement in any church—at best, these are, as far as I know, nominal believers.
3. Those who are believers in Christ, study their Bibles, pray, and even reach out in loving service, yet have no commitment to any particular church or ecclesial community. They may attend or retain membership in some denomination or tradition, but for them, the Christian faith consists of an individual's relationship with Jesus Christ.

4. Those who, by grace, have discovered and surrendered in faith to Jesus Christ (though they are far from perfect Christians), who either have become or have always been active members of the Church, and who, by grace, are trying to continue on as faithful members of the Body of Christ.

As I thought about these groups, it struck me that it all had to do with *being* and *abiding*.

Being in Christ

Our Lord desires that every person first comes to live by faith *in Him*. Our Lord told His followers, as well as anyone hearing Him who might be struggling to understand who He was, "No one comes to the Father, but by me" (Jn 14:6). He also said, "In that day [i.e., after His death and Resurrection] you will know that I am in my Father, and *you in me, and I in you*" (Jn 14:20).[1]

We are those who live "in that day" and therefore are called to be *in Him* and *He in us*, but what does this mean? How does it happen? Scripture teaches that, normally, a person comes to live *in Christ* through baptism and faith, but sometimes only by faith, if a person has not been told about the necessity of baptism.

At first glance, it might seem from some Scripture texts that only *believing* is necessary. As our Lord said to the multitudes who had followed Him after being miraculously fed with five barley loaves, "For this is the will of my Father, that every one who sees the Son and *believes* in him should have eternal life; and I will raise him up at the last day" (Jn 6:40). There's also that familiar text, "For God so loved the world that he gave his only-begotten Son, that whoever *believes* in him should not perish but have eternal life" (Jn 3:16). Within the context, however, of all of our Lord's teachings and the entire New

---

[1] Throughout this chapter, any italicized emphasis in Scripture citations has been added.

Testament, it becomes apparent that it was assumed that all adults who came to *believe in Christ* were then baptized *into Christ*, *into* His Body, the Church. As Saint Paul wrote, "[F]or *in Christ Jesus*, you are all sons of God, through faith. For as many of you as were baptized *into Christ* have *put on Christ*" (Gal 3:26–27).

This assumption of the necessity of baptism is confirmed outside the New Testament in the writings of the earliest Church writers. For example, Saint Justin Martyr, a convert from Platonic philosophy, wrote in his *First Apology*, around the year 150:

> Through Christ we received new life and we consecrated ourselves to God. I will explain the way in which we did this. Those who believe what we teach is true and who give assurance of their ability to live according to that teaching are taught to ask God's forgiveness for their sins by prayer and fasting, and we pray and fast with them. We then lead them to a place where there is water and they are reborn in the same way as we were reborn; that is to say, they are washed in the water in the name of God, the Father and the Lord of the whole universe, of our Savior Jesus Christ and of the Holy Spirit. This is done because Christ said: Unless you are born again you will not enter the kingdom of heaven.[2]

Our Lord desires that every person be *in Him*. This is what drives the need of all Christians to share the gospel with every person in their lives: "Him we proclaim, warning every man and teaching every man in all wisdom, that we may present every man mature *in Christ*" (Col 1:28).

This baptismal entrance *into Christ* changes us. As Saint Paul reminded the Corinthian believers, "Therefore, if any one is *in Christ*, he is a new creation; the old has passed away, behold, the new has come" (2 Cor 5:17). To the Roman believers, he wrote, "There is therefore now no condemnation for those who are *in Christ Jesus*" (8:1). Saint Paul reminded the Ephesian believers that through their baptismal entrance *into Christ*, alluded to by the terms he used, they were "sealed with the promised Holy Spirit" (1:13), "having the eyes of [their] hearts enlightened" (1:18).

---

[2] Justin Martyr, *First Apology*, chap. 61, in Johannes Quasten, ed., *Florilegium Patristicum*, 14–16; quoted in *Liturgy of the Hours*, vol. 2 (New York: Catholic Book Publishing, 1976), 720.

Very early in the life of the Church, this new birth through baptism was granted to every member of the family (see Acts 16:33),
even newborns. Though infants obviously could not place their
faith in Christ, their believing and baptized parents willingly took
responsibility for ensuring that their baptized children would learn
the meaning of their baptisms and their Christian faith. In time, this
infant baptismal rebirth was recognized as the New Covenant equiv-
alent to the Old Covenant requirement of circumcision.

This *being in Christ*, however, is only the beginning of the Christian life, and though many Christians believe that this beginning is
all that matters (i.e., "once saved, always saved"), Scripture teaches
otherwise.

Abiding in Christ

Our Lord warned His followers that they must *abide* (remain, continue) *in Him*:

> *Abide in me, and I in you.* As the branch cannot bear fruit by itself,
> unless it *abides* in the vine, neither can you, unless you *abide in me.*
> I am the vine, you are the branches. He who *abides in me, and I in*
> *him*, he it is that bears much fruit, *for apart from me you can do nothing.*
> If a man does not *abide in me*, he is cast forth as a branch and with-
> ers; and the branches are gathered, thrown into the fire and burned.
> (Jn 15:4–6)

In other words, *being in Christ* is the beginning, but not the end;
nor is it all that is necessary. As I mentioned in an earlier chapter,
when our Lord told the apostle John to write to the seven churches
under his care, He promised future and eternal blessings, but only
to those who "conquer" (Rev 2:2ff.). Even more telling, our Lord
ended the book of Revelation with this chilling warning:

> And he who sat upon the throne said, "Behold, I make all things
> new." Also he said, "Write this, for these words are trustworthy and
> true." And he said to me, "It is done! I am the Alpha and the Omega,
> the beginning and the end. To the thirsty I will give water without
> price from the fountain of the water of life. He who conquers shall

have this heritage, and I will be his God and he shall be my son. But as for the cowardly, the faithless, the polluted, as for murderers, fornicators, sorcerers, idolaters, and all liars, their lot shall be in the lake that burns with fire and brimstone, which is the second death. (21:5–8)

The images here are important: "the thirsty", who are granted the "water of life", are those who believe and through baptism are enlightened and are now *in Christ*; those then who *conquer* are those who, strengthened by grace, have *abided in Christ* to the end. Those who do not abide in Christ, who turn from God and live in sin, are those who will suffer "the second death".

The First Letter of John particularly emphasized the necessity of abiding in Christ. For example, Saint John wrote in 2:24, "Let what you heard from the beginning *abide* in you. If what you heard from the beginning *abides* in you, then you will *abide in the Son and in the Father.*" In 2:28, he also wrote, "And now, little children, *abide in him*, so that when he appears we may have confidence and not shrink from him in shame at his coming."

How do we abide (remain, continue) in Christ? Essentially, this is what most of the New Testament is about. Nearly every New Testament epistle was written to Christian believers who through baptism were already *in Christ*. Saints Paul, Peter, James, John, and Jude were not trying to convert them but rather reminding them of their need to abide in Christ. Put simply, abiding in Him means living out our belief in Him, which is essentially what is meant by *believing*. Our Lord also described this simply as "following" Him (see Mk 1:17; 8:34; 10:21). Following, believing, or abiding in Him requires that we abide in His Word, that we obediently align our lives with His teaching and as a result produce the fruits of virtues and holiness (see Jn 15:7–8). As Jesus told the Jews He was calling to follow Him, "If you *continue* [*abide*] in my word, you are truly my disciples, and you will know the truth, and the truth will make you free" (Jn 8:31–32).

His Word, however, is not limited to the Scriptures alone but includes the full Deposit of Faith as delivered by Him to His apostles and preserved by the Holy Spirit in the Church.

It is crucial to understand that believing in Christ is more than a mental assent to the existence of the trinitarian God and the other truths passed down from Christ through His apostles and the Church to us; believing involves obedience to what this truth requires of us. More statements from the apostle John's first letter elucidate this—in 3:24: "All who keep his commandments *abide in him, and he in them.* And by this we know that *he abides in us,* by the Spirit which he has given us"; and 2:6: "He who says he *abides in him* ought to walk in the same way in which he walked."

These verses are particularly relevant when one recognizes that being in and abiding in Christ are a living out by grace of our baptismal regeneration, our rebirth as sons and daughters of God, into the family of God, the Church: "we have passed out of death" (1 Jn 3:14) and are now called to abide in Him and His Word.

There is, though, only one place in all of Scripture where our Lord specifically explained how His disciples can abide in Him, and that is in His discourse on His Body and Blood:

> So Jesus said to them, "Truly, truly, I say to you, unless you eat the flesh of the Son of man and drink his blood, *you have no life in you;* he who eats my flesh and drinks my blood *has eternal life,* and I will raise him up at the last day. For my flesh is food indeed, and my blood is drink indeed. *He who eats my flesh and drinks my blood abides in me, and I in him.* (Jn 6:53–56)

Here our Lord explains that eternal life is something that believers will experience not only after death but now in this life, which is precisely what being in and abiding in Christ mean.

We come to dwell in Him through the sacrament of baptism, and we abide in Him (continue in union with Him) and experience the blessings of eternal life now through the gift of the Eucharist. This is why being in and abiding in Christ presume active membership in the Church, for it is through the ministry of the Church that we are baptized and receive the graces of the sacraments that enable us to abide in Him. As Pope Francis recently said:

> The Christian is not a baptized person that receives Baptism and then goes along his own way. The first fruit of Baptism is to make yourself belong to the Church, to the people of God. A Christian without a Church is not understood. And for this reason, the great Paul VI said that it is an absurd dichotomy to love Christ without the Church; to

listen to Christ but not the Church; to be with Christ at the edge of the Church. It can't be done. It is an absurd dichotomy.[3]

Abiding in Christ is a lifelong quest, with the aid of grace, to work out our salvation with fear and trembling, in imitation of Saint Paul, as he sought to imitate Christ (see Phil 2:12; 1 Cor 11:1). For this, we must never fall into the danger of presumption, for as Saint Paul also warned, "Therefore let any one who thinks that he stands take heed lest he fall. No temptation has overtaken you that is not common to man. God is faithful, and he will not let you be tempted beyond your strength, but with the temptation will also provide the way of escape, that you may be able to endure it" (1 Cor 10:12–13).

Consequently, each one of us is always in need of further evangelism, further awakening, further submitting to the love of Christ—further growth in holiness—for it is only then that we can be vessels of grace for sharing what we have received with others.

Loving

But there is more to this analogy, for being and abiding are only the first two stages of the journey; there is a necessary third stage.

After you've commenced being on a farm, or "bought the farm", as the phrase goes in another context (with the wisdom of hindsight), the challenge is to continue abiding on the farm, replacing that long list of vices with virtues, improving and developing the property, its livestock, and produce. Hopefully, this means that you and your family are becoming more and more productive. This is the utopian view of farming, of course, and why having bought the farm has become synonymous with death. What keeps a farmer and his family going are not just fear or lack of alternatives, but mostly love—for life on the farm, the work, the culture (agri*culture*), the nearness to God's creation, even love for the freedom of dependence on His providence. This is ultimately what makes a farmer *be* a farmer and *remain*

---

[3] "Pope Francis: A Christian without the Church Is 'an Absurd Dichotomy'", January 30, 2014, Zenit, http://www.zenit.org/en/articles/pope-francis-a-christian-without-the-church-is-an-absurd-dichotomy.

a farmer and inspires his children to remain in farming; if this love is lost, so goes the family farm and, as Thomas Jefferson and hundreds of others have said since, so goes our nation.

In the middle of His Sermon on the Mount, Jesus warned His listeners: "Enter by the narrow gate; for the gate is wide and the way is easy, that leads to destruction, and those who enter by it are many. For the gate is narrow and the way is hard, that leads to life, and those who find it are few" (Mt 7:13–14).

Interspersed throughout the fences that surround and subdivide the fields of our rural land are a variety of gates, from those wide enough to allow a tractor with implements to pass through down to one barely wide enough to allow my own aging girth. Some gates are made narrow to control who or what can pass through them. If I open one of our wider gates with my cattle crowded behind me, they could push by me, maybe not to destruction, but at least to my dismay. Other gates, on the other hand, are narrow because of the constricting surroundings—closely packed trees or buildings, or a narrow rocky gorge—and a herd of cattle by necessity must constrict itself down to single file to squeeze through, and even then, tightly and patiently.

Within the context of our entire faith, the narrow gate to which our Lord refers is not merely a small gate through which we pass if we believe and "confess with our lips" (Rom 10:9) the correct doctrine about Jesus, as if with a password or a magical incantation. Rather, the gate of salvation is narrow because it stands at the constricted end of a long narrowing journey of abiding in Christ. The journey begins with being in Him through faith and baptism and continues through a narrowing of life and our attachments through the "obedience of faith", as Saint Paul puts it in Romans 1:5. In this abiding, our attachments to the world, to sin, and to ourselves need to be broken—like a herd of cattle narrowing down to single file—as our focus becomes more and more on Christ. This process of detachment, a perceived narrowing, is yet a growing in joy, which was the reason our Lord told His followers about their need to abide: "that my joy may be in you, and that your joy may be full" (Jn 15:11).

This joy grows as we grow in the necessary third stage of *loving in Christ*, for we are being and abiding in Christ only to the extent that we are growing in love for God and others. We may believe in God and become an adopted child in the family; we may have cleaned up our lives by grace and appear as saints in the eyes of others. But God sees more deeply into our soul, heart, and conscience, behind our actions, and He is looking for signs of love. This is why the First Letter of John is such an important and deeply spiritual gem in the New Testament. Writing to believers who already had been anointed with the Holy Spirit through baptism and were striving to abide in Christ by grace, he reminded them that there was more:

> We know that we have passed out of death into life, because we love the brethren. He who does not love *abides* in death. (3:14, RSV)

> But if any one has the world's goods and sees his brother in need, yet closes his heart against him, how does God's love *abide in him?* (3:17)

> No man has ever seen God; if we love one another, God *abides* in us and his love is perfected in us. By this we know that we *abide* in him and he in us, because he has given us of his own Spirit. (4:12–13)

> Whoever confesses that Jesus is the Son of God, God *abides* in him, and he in God. So we know and believe the love God has for us. God is love, and he who *abides* in love *abides* in God, and God *abides* in him. (4:15–16)

As Saint Paul wrote in that familiar passage, so often read or sung at weddings but too often quickly forgotten, "So faith, hope, love *abide*, these three; but the greatest of these is *love*" (1 Cor 13:13). The evidence of these three virtues was a sign to Saint Paul that the believers at Colossae were *abiding* and *loving in Christ*: "We always thank God, the Father of our Lord Jesus Christ, when we pray for you, because we have heard of your *faith* in Christ Jesus and of the *love* which you have for all the saints, because of the *hope* laid up for you in heaven" (Col 1:3–5).

If, by grace, we one day stand poised to enter through that narrow gate and pause to consider the journey, we will discover that the long narrowing road that began widely with *being* and continued its narrowing through *abiding* was, in fact, always the road of *loving*. This is essentially what the Church teaches when she declares that "even though incorporated into the Church, one who does not however persevere in charity is not saved."[4]

This being said, I thought back on those four groups of friends I mentioned earlier. I certainly can never know where anyone is in relation to Christ and His Church, especially because I myself am such an imperfect example of being, abiding, and especially loving. In what ways, therefore, can these friends of ours be categorized in relation to whether they are in Christ, abiding in Him, and loving in Him to the end?

1. Those who are neither *in Christ*, through baptism or faith, nor *abiding in Christ* through active membership in the Church

The Church teaches, in obedience to the wide open arms of our merciful, loving Lord, that

> those who have not yet received the Gospel are related to the People of God in various ways.... The plan of salvation also includes those who acknowledge the Creator.... Nor is God remote from those who in shadows and images seek the unknown God, since he gives to all men life and breath and all things (cf. Acts 17:25–28), and since the Savior wills all men to be saved.... [Therefore,] those who, through no fault of their own, do not know the Gospel of Christ or his Church, but who nevertheless seek God with a sincere heart, and, moved by grace, try in their actions to do his will as they know it through the dictates of their conscience—those too may achieve eternal salvation.[5]

Consequently, though our non-Christian friends and family may never have placed their faith in Christ and lived in Him, they may have responded in love to the merciful voice of Christ in their consciences. Therefore, we entrust them into the merciful hands of Christ.

---

[4] *Catechism of the Catholic Church* (*CCC*), 2nd ed. (Vatican City: Libreria Editrice Vaticana, 1997), no. 837, quoting Second Vatican Council, *Lumen Gentium*, no. 14.

[5] *Lumen Gentium*, no. 16; cf. 1 Tim 2:4.

Dorothy Day expressed it this way in her first telling of her conversion story:

> It is impossible for any one of those who has real charity in his heart not to serve Christ. Even some of those who think they hate Him, have consecrated their lives to Him; for Jesus is disguised and masked in the midst of men, hidden among the poor, among the sick, among prisoners, among strangers. Many who serve Him officially have never known who He was, and many who do tho even know His name, will hear on the last day the words that open to them the gates of joy.[6]

However, given what the Church says about these friends of ours, we must not presume on this hopeful outcome, for we also know that our Lord warned that apart from Him we can do nothing (see Jn 15:5) and that those who find the narrow gate are few (see Mt 7:14). So we must do what our Lord has called us to do: "Go therefore and make disciples of all nations, baptizing them in the name of the Father and of the Son and of the Holy Spirit" (Mt 28:19). We don't stand in judgment of anyone, for God in His mercy can save anyone through Christ and His Church, even if they know neither; rather, we are called to speak the truth of Christ boldly to them in love (see Eph 4:25).

2. Those who have been baptized *into Christ* but, by all outward appearances, are not *abiding in Him*

These are fallen-away or nominal Christians, for whom the Church has called for a New Evangelization. Many of these nominal Christians presume that, once having been baptized into Christ or once having "accepted Christ as their personal Savior", they are now guaranteed salvation, regardless of how they abide. Even though Saint Paul did say that the gift of the Holy Spirit through baptism is "the guarantee of our inheritance until we acquire possession of it" (Eph 1:14), this does not mean that this initial entrance into Christ guarantees that we will abide in Christ throughout our lives. As the author of Hebrews warned:

---

[6]Dorothy Day, *From Union Square to Rome* (Maryknoll, N.Y.: Orbis Books, 2006), 11.

> For it is impossible [humanly speaking, that is, for nothing is impossible for God] to restore again to repentance those who have once been enlightened [i.e., baptized into Christ], who have tasted the heavenly gift, and have become partakers of the Holy Spirit, and have tasted the goodness of the word of God and the powers of the age to come, if they then commit apostasy, since they crucify the Son of God on their own account and hold him up to contempt. (6:4–6)

This is why Christ warned His followers that being in Him was not enough; we must abide in Him, which is why nominal or fallen-away baptized Christians, of all people, need to be evangelized, for they may be the hardest to reach. They may have squandered the greatest gift they have been given. It certainly is possible that before the end they may respond in love to the voice of Christ in their consciences, but if not, when they stand before their Creator, they may be held more accountable for this rejection of Christ than those who have never known Him.

3. Those who faithfully believe in Jesus Christ and seek to serve Him in love—who may or may not have been *baptized* into Christ—yet *abide in Him* as independent Christians, and therefore imperfectly through separation from His Church and her sacraments

These baptized or unbaptized faithful Christians are indeed members of the Mystical Body of Christ, but imperfectly, and therefore they need to be evangelized "for the sake of their salvation". This is not a matter of having a name on a membership roll but rather a matter of abiding fully in Christ and coming to know the true meaning of love.

Since our Lord warned that apart from Him we can do nothing (Jn 15:5), and Saint Paul emphasized that the Church is the "Body of Christ" (Eph 1:22–23) and "the pillar and bulwark of the truth" (1 Tim 3:15), the surest way we are united with Him is through active communion with our baptized brothers and sisters in worship, prayer, service, and especially through participation in the sacraments, particularly through the communion of His Body and Blood.

What is most crucial, however, is that we need this communion to learn what love truly is. Many well-meaning, sincere Christians fail to recognize that true Christ-centered love requires suffering, sacrifice, and self-denial. When I was a Presbyterian pastor, I emphasized how we had been mercifully granted by grace to believe in Him, yet I was oblivious of the second half of the equation. As Saint Paul proclaimed, "For it has been granted to you that for the sake of Christ you should not only believe in him *but also suffer for his sake*" (Phil 1:29). Without the boundaries of the Church's teachings, individual Christians can be moved by so many voices that they develop their own images of love, as we see being done today by too many denominations, voting democratically to widen that narrow gate into a six-lane expressway, all in the name of "love".

For these fellow Christian brothers and sisters, the Church has called for a unique form of evangelism called *dialogue*. Recognizing the many things that unite us, we are called to stand, not above, but beside them in love and service, united in prayer and suffering, sharing with them the fullness of the truth that we have mercifully received as a gift of grace.

4. Those who through baptism and faith are *in Christ*, and who, through both sacramental and actual graces, are *abiding in Christ* and striving to grow in *love* as active members of the Church

I suppose I consider myself in this group, though as I quoted Saint Paul earlier, I have certainly not "already obtained this or am already perfect; but I press on to make it my own, because Christ Jesus has made me his own" (Phil 3:12). This is why Saint Paul also emphasized that the narrowing down of our lives in obedience to Christ, through being, abiding, and loving, leading to the joy that Christ promised, involves "forgetting what lies behind and straining forward to what lies ahead, [pressing] on toward the goal for the prize of the upward call of God in Christ Jesus" (Phil 3:13–14). However, he wasn't just speaking to beginners on the journey, to the young and inexperienced who had just "bought the farm" and were struggling with the mere fundamentals. He was speaking to old codgers like me, and maybe you, for he wrote, "Let those of us who are mature be thus minded; and if in anything you are otherwise minded, God will reveal that also to you. Only let us hold true to what we have attained. Brethren, join in imitating me, and mark those who so walk as you have an example in us" (Phil 3:15–17).

What is most important, though, is that we never cease praying for our friends, living or departed, for God's mercy extends far beyond the boundaries of time. He works in ways we might never know, but what we have seen in the lives of those around us must be a reminder of our own imminent need of being, abiding, and loving in Christ. As the author of Hebrews wrote:

> Therefore, since we are surrounded by so great a cloud of witnesses, let us also lay aside every weight, and sin which clings so closely, and let us run with perseverance the race that is set before us, looking to Jesus the pioneer and perfecter of our faith, who for the joy that was set before him endured the cross, despising the shame, and is seated at the right hand of the throne of God. (12:1–2)

14

Inch by Inch, Row by Row

Blessed are the poor in spirit, for theirs is the kingdom of heaven.

—Matthew 5:3

I'm looking once again at our fairly large—or, should I say, ambitious—garden.

Last year, I staked it out: eighty by twenty feet, along a slightly south-facing slope, a convenient fifty feet from our house. I then used the rototiller attachment on my tractor sev-

eral times to prepare the soil. My son Richard helped me shovel and transfer four wheelbarrow loads of aged cow manure from the barn and distribute it across the garden, which led to more passes with the rototiller, until the garden was primed and ready for planting. Using a hand cultivator, I spent most of an afternoon and long into the evening pulling the dirt into mounds and raised beds to hold our planned crops: sweet corn, watermelons, muskmelons, zucchini, squash, string beans, cucumbers, tomatoes, peppers, several varieties of lettuce, and a special patch of zinnias for Marilyn.

As I planted, I found myself mindlessly singing one of my favorite old songs, from my folk-singing days in the sixties, "Garden Song", written by David Mallett and recorded by many. You remember: "Inch by inch, row by row, I'm gonna make this garden grow; all it takes is a rake and a hoe and a piece of fertile ground",[1] et cetera, et cetera. The theology of the song ain't perfect, but it kept me going, fighting the heat and humidity.

After this initial great start, the garden took off. The raised beds protected the plants from our usual Ohio "frog stranglers", as Marilyn calls our downpours. The plants grew, and for several weeks it looked as if, for the first time in my life, I actually had planted a successful garden!

But then trips started filling my work schedule, and my mother's health began failing, which required more time away. Consequently the unwanted plants—the weeds—and the uninvited guests—the deer, the rabbits, and our free-range chickens—conspired to overpower, subdue, and conquer. By grace, we gleaned our fair share of everything, but it took wading, burrowing, and searching to find the fruit among the chaff.

Now a year later, the garden is set to start growing. I've rototilled, fertilized, mounded, planted, and even cultivated once again to fend away the invaders. But what will this garden be like come August or September?

One Day at a Time for a Lifetime

Throughout this book, I've talked about the need to live each day as if it's our last. We have no natural, divine right to a long life; what we've experienced has been a gift, and we should be grateful for every day, even through sorrow, sadness, failure, and frustration.

Long ago, Thomas à Kempis said it well:

> You should order your every deed and thought as though today were the day of your death. Had you a good conscience,

---

[1] David Mallett, "Garden Song", BMG Music, Cherry Lane Music Publishing Company.

death would hold no terrors for you; even so, it were better to avoid sin than to escape death. If you are not ready to die today, will tomorrow find you better prepared?

Blessed is the man who keeps the hour of his death always in mind, and daily prepares himself to die. Each morning remember that you may but live until evening; and in the evening, do not presume to promise yourself another day. Be ready at all times, and so live that death may never find you unprepared.

Happy and wise is he who endeavours to be during his life as he wishes to be found at his death. For these things will afford us sure hope of a happy death: perfect contempt of the world; fervent desire to grow in holiness; love of discipline; the practice of penance; ready obedience; self-denial; the bearing of every trial for the love of Christ.[2]

Everything expressed in this book has been about being, abiding, and loving in Christ, every day, in every present moment. How we handle the normal hurdles of life, in Christ, will determine our passage from this life to the next: "For we must all appear before the judgment seat of Christ, so that each one may receive good or evil, according to what he has done in the body" (2 Cor 5:10). And since we never know when this event might occur, we are called to be ready daily. "Watch therefore, for you do not know on what day your Lord is coming" (Mt 24:42). It could be before you finish reading this page.

The truth is, though, that most of us will live longer than that. Most of us will live for months, even years, on into an increasingly unpredictable future. How are we to prepare for this, for living every day as if it's our last, for possibly ten, twenty, or more years—and not just for ourselves, but for and with our spouse and family?

Again, as I've expressed several times before, I believe it helps to remember that, as persons created in the image of God, we are both body and spirit. We are not mere biological beings, as the scientific materialistic atheists would tell us, destined to become nothing but fertilizer when we die, an insignificant part "in nature's chain",[3] replenishing "Mother Earth"[4] with what we irresponsibly took from

[2] Thomas à Kempis, *The Imitation of Christ* (New York: Penguin Books, 1982), 57–58.
[3] David Mallett, "Garden Song", verse 2, line 6.
[4] Ibid., verse 3, line 3.

her. Nor are we just heavenly spirits trapped in earthly bodies, such that only the destiny of our souls matters. Rather, we are both, which is why our faith has always emphasized the resurrection of the body: at death, our souls face a first, personal judgment; meanwhile our bodies remain in the ground, decaying, maybe for centuries, until our souls and bodies are reunited in the general resurrection on Judgment Day.

Living each day as if it is our last means keeping our souls in grace, clean of sin and free from the attachments to this world that we gain through the senses of our bodies. But since, according to God's providence, we may be gifted with decades of living, we must be good stewards of these bodies, so that our whole being, body and soul, can flourish in faith, hope, and love. As discussed earlier, for this to happen we must provide the bodily goods (food, liquids, clothing, shelter) we need so that our entire person can thrive. At the same time, we must strive to become less attached to unnecessary external goods because, like the weeds and uninvited critters that took over my garden last year, attachments can conspire to overpower, subdue, and conquer us, body and soul.

In determining what specific actions we need to take—daily and for years to come—we must recognize that salvation is not an individualistic quest. We are called to be faithful individuals within the Body of Christ, the Church. Our call to love our neighbor as Christ loved us means that we are called, therefore, not only to be ready ourselves, but to do all we can to help our neighbors live today as if it is their last day—to be ready spiritually to meet God. Are they living in grace? Are their souls pure?

But this means recognizing that we and our neighbors—we and our families—may be living together for a long time! How can we help each other without becoming burdens to each other? Certainly, we're called to help and care for each other, yet we can't presume on this—we can't merely assume that if we get sick or disabled, our children will pick up the slack. A glutton or a hoarder robs from the bodily goods of others, eventually becoming a burden on them through neglected health and accumulated attachments, and when he dies, such a person leaves behind an irresponsible burden of unnecessary goods. This means that each of us ought to live healthful, simple, selfless lives, so that if one day we have no choice but to be a "burden", we will be as little of a burden as possible—maybe even a blessing.

A Staircase to Conversion

Looking at the present beauty of my garden, knowing the effort it will take every day for months to come, I'm reminded of the new gospel that our Lord gave to those who desired to grow closer to Him and thereby enter the kingdom. He gave this in a sermon on a mount of grass, out in a field, to people gathered around Him, enjoying the wind and the sun, the songs of birds and the camaraderie of family and friends.

Jesus talked about being blessed, about the qualities that this requires, and about rewards. We've all heard these Beatitudes, and usually they're interpreted as separate promises referring, possibly, to separate groups of individuals:

> Blessed are the poor in spirit, for theirs is the kingdom of heaven.
> Blessed are those who mourn, for they shall be comforted.
> Blessed are the meek, for they shall inherit the earth.
> Blessed are those who hunger and thirst for righteousness, for they shall be satisfied.
> Blessed are the merciful, for they shall obtain mercy.
> Blessed are the pure in heart, for they shall see God.
> Blessed are the peacemakers, for they shall be called sons of God.
> Blessed are those who are persecuted for righteousness' sake, for theirs is the kingdom of heaven.
> Blessed are you when men revile you and persecute you and utter all kinds of evil against you falsely on my account. Rejoice and be glad, for your reward is great in heaven, for so men persecuted the prophets who were before you. (Mt 5:3–12)

Years ago in my readings, I discovered the writings of a fourth-century bishop, Saint Chromatius of Aquileia (A.D. 340–408). He was a contemporary and friend of Saints Augustine, Ambrose, and Jerome. He preached something about these Beatitudes that I had never heard but that was understood by many of the early Fathers of the Church. In a sermon on Matthew, Chromatius wrote:

> Our Lord, Our savior, establishes extremely solid steps of precious stones, by which saintly souls and faithful can climb, can rise to this supreme good, which is the kingdom of heaven.... Brethren, before your eyes are the eight rungs of the gospel, constructed, as I have said,

with precious stones. Behold Jacob's ladder which starts on earth and whose top touches heaven. He who climbs it finds the gate of heaven, and having entered it, will have endless joy in the presence of the Lord, eternally praising Him with the holy angels.[5]

Another contemporary of Saint Chromatius, Saint Gregory of Nyssa (330–395), the brother of Saint Basil the Great, also promoted this view. Whereas Saint Chromatius wrote as a Western Latin Catholic bishop, Saint Gregory was an Eastern Greek Catholic bishop. There is no evidence that they ever communicated, and Saint Gregory's sermons on the Beatitudes may even have predated those of Saint Chromatius. Here is how Saint Gregory introduces this concept:

When one climbs up by a ladder, he sets foot on the first step, and from there goes on to the one above. Again the second step carries the climber up to the third, and this to the following, and hence to the next. Thus the person who goes up always ascends from where he is to the step above until he reaches the top of his ascent. Now why do I begin like this? It seems to me that the Beatitudes are arranged in order like so many steps, so as to facilitate the ascent from one to the other. For if a man's mind has ascended to the first Beatitude, he will accept what follows as a necessary result of thought, even though the next clause seems to say something new beyond what had been said in the first.[6]

Pope Saint Leo the Great (d. 461), a generation later, confirmed this idea of the Beatitudes as a staircase of conversion in his own sermon on the Beatitudes: "Thus whoever longs to attain eternal blessedness can now recognize the steps that lead to that high happiness."[7]

Jesus was not only saying that God blesses those who find themselves impotently in a state of poverty, mourning, meekness, et cetera, but He was commanding His hearers willingly to choose poverty of spirit, et cetera. From the perspective of Saints Chromatius, Gregory

[5] Saint Chromatius of Aquileia, "Sermon on the Beatitudes", quoted in *Glimpses of the Church Fathers*, by Claire Russell (London: Scepter Press, 1996), 215, 219.

[6] Saint Gregory of Nyssa, *St. Gregory of Nyssa: The Lord's Prayer, and the Beatitudes*, trans. Hilda C. Graef (New York: Paulist Press, 1954), 97.

[7] Pope Saint Leo the Great, Sermon 95, "A Homily on the Beatitudes", quoted in *Liturgy of the Hours,* vol. 4, 22nd week, Thursday, Office of Readings, 207.

of Nyssa, and Leo the Great, Jesus was telling His followers that each Beatitude was a step or rung that leads to the next and therefore becomes a foundation for the next. Each step yields a reward yet also entails a crisis (either an obstacle to moving forward or a temptation to fall back), for each step requires sacrifice, perseverance, and choosing to actualize the grace available.

While this certainly deserves a more thorough discussion, here we have room only for a fairly simple one. The first step, "blessed are the poor in spirit", refers to detachment from the world, and therefore choosing an attachment to Jesus Christ. Here is a poverty that we choose, regardless of material wealth or condition in life. Though certainly not always the case, there are poor people who sadly envy what others have. There are also rich folk who recognize that everything they have is a gift from God for which they are eternally responsible, and therefore they focus on filling the needs of the poor. This poverty of spirit involves seeing life from the perspective of God the Father: material things are good in themselves, but not as ends; they are only fleeting and of no eternal value.

This first step involves essentially what the first disciples did: "Immediately they left their nets and followed him" (Mt 4:20). All of Jesus' instructions on discipleship begin here, and one must not turn back: "No one who puts his hand to the plow and looks back is fit for the kingdom of God" (Lk 9:62).

The reward for detachment from the kingdom of this world is "the kingdom of heaven". A crisis can arise, however, when a person starts to "mourn" for the things he has left behind or could have had. We can fall back, through our choices, to our old attachments, or we can willingly, by grace, choose to move to the next step.

Step 2 ("Blessed are those who mourn") involves detachment from sin in obedience to Jesus Christ: mourning over the way the sins to which we have become attached have separated us from God and from becoming the people He created us to be. The reward for remorse and repentance is being "comforted", or having an inner affirmation of being forgiven, cleansed by grace—becoming new creations by grace. A crisis can arise, however, from our pride, when we second-guess the need to change and instead regress into sin. This was why Saint Paul warned the newly baptized pagan converts in Ephesus not to fall back into their former sinful lifestyles but exhorted them: "Put off the old man that belongs to your former manner of life and is corrupt through deceitful lusts, and be renewed in the spirit of your minds, and put on the new man, created after the likeness of God in true righteousness and holiness" (4:22–24).

After one has detached himself from this world and from sin, he proceeds to step 3 ("Blessed are the meek"), which involves detachment from self: choosing humbly to be like Jesus. When we let go of ourselves as the center of our own universes and trust in God's providence, He literally promises us the world ("for they shall inherit the earth"). But a crisis can arise if we once again "hunger and thirst" for the attention we once had when we were the center and focus of our lives. We can fall back, seeking the attention and praise of others, or we can willingly, by grace, choose to put others first—seeking their good, for the sake of Christ—and by grace move to the next step.

Being detached from the world, sin, and ourselves, we can attain the fourth step, in which, by grace, we "hunger and thirst for righteousness". Jesus promises that if we respond to and attach ourselves to this inner longing for holiness, we "shall be satisfied"; we will be changed by grace. A crisis can arise, though, when we discover that this requires more sacrifice—that we are to forgive and show mercy, even to those/who hurt or hate us. We can fall back by refusing to love and forgive, by returning to love of self over others, by returning to sinful behavior rather than listening to anyone else, and by attaching ourselves again to things of this world. Or we can ask God for the grace necessary to help us choose to love, to forgive, regardless of how we feel. This leads to the next step.

Step 5 ("Blessed are the merciful") involves willingly obeying and living out righteousness: loving as Christ has loved us. The reward is that we in turn receive and experience God's mercy. A crisis can arise when we are tempted to feel bitterness for letting go of what we consider justice: when we regret letting go of punishing someone who has hurt us. We can harbor within our hearts bitterness because we have shown love, forgiveness, and mercy toward those we feel deserve rejection, punishment, and justice. This bitterness can build within our hearts until we quench the Spirit, stepping backward into self, into sin, and away from God. Or we can repent of this sinfulness of heart, asking God to cleanse our hearts of whatever turns us away from Him, praying as David once did, "Create in me a clean heart, O God, and put a new and right spirit within me" (Ps 51:10). This leads us to the next step.

As a result of willingly detaching ourselves, aided by grace, from the world, sin, and self, hungering and thirsting instead for righteousness, and living this out in mercy toward others, our hearts become changed and purified ("Blessed are the pure in heart"). The reward for this is the gift of seeing God. The great Christian spiritual writers of both the East and the West have understood the gift of seeing God as the intimacy of contemplation. A pure heart is one that has been cleansed of the distractions of the world, the flesh, and the devil and, by grace, is able to experience the journey of the three ways of the spiritual life, particularly the passive purgation of the senses and the spirit, leading to an intimate union with Christ.

A crisis can arise here, however, through the possibility of isolation. Up to this point, all of the steps have the potential of tempting a person into a self-preserving isolation. As a result of our efforts to detach ourselves from the world, sin, and self, followed by a concentrated hunger and thirst for righteousness and then a desire to be loving and merciful to everyone who crosses our path, we may in actuality have cornered ourselves into an exodus from the world, an inward focusing on ourselves; even a resentful privatization of our spiritual lives, leading to bitterness whenever anyone has the "insensitive gall" to interfere, to intrude upon our "superior" efforts at holiness! Or we can respond malleably to the implications and call of the first six steps, following in obedience their trajectory out from ourselves, following the example of Christ, out into the world, and on to the next step.

Beatitude 7 involves imitating Christ in the world by being a peacemaker ("Blessed are the peacemakers"). This means becoming not so much a skilled negotiator or arbiter between warring peoples but rather a willing messenger of Jesus in the lives of others. The reward for stepping out in obedience to live out the implications of these steps in the relationships that God has given us—in our marriages, families, neighborhoods, parishes, workplaces, et cetera—is that people might recognize us as indeed "sons of God". They might be moved to see our good works and give glory to God the Father (see Mt 5:16).

They might not, however, and this could bring about a crisis. They might react negatively to our efforts, maybe even turn against us in ridicule or persecution. We can respond by backing off. We can return to the safety of our self-focused corner to seek holiness in isolation. Or worse, we can begin doubting, even rejecting the previous stages, giving in to the criticism of the crowd by joining their ranks. We can begin desiring their acceptance over the desire for righteousness until we have stepped so far backward that we are once again attached to seeking what is "best" for ourselves, to sin and the world. Or, by grace, we can accept the suffering that comes from standing up for what is right and good, pure and true, and this leads to the next step.

Here, by grace, we have become willing to accept the persecution that comes from defending truth ("Blessed are those who are persecuted for righteousness' sake"). Those who react in ridicule might not realize why we are doing this (or in Whose Name we are doing this); they might merely be reacting against our pointing out, even if done in love, their failure to do what is true, good, and pure. Our reward? At this stage, we might expect by now an exalted, glorious reward, but in fact we receive what we were promised in step 1: membership in the kingdom. In other words, being persecuted for doing what is right is par for the course: this is our duty as members of the Body of Christ. But then again, what is greater than eternal membership in the Family of God?

This can bring on a crisis, however, when others reject, ridicule, or persecute not just the moral or ethical imperatives of our efforts but our religious convictions and motives: they might ridicule our Lord and cast aspersions on our Christian faith. We can respond by backing off and, like Simon Peter, denying our Lord and our faith—maybe only in a subtle way; maybe only by slighting the underlying motivating significance of our religious convictions; maybe by declaring that we are doing this not because Jesus says so or because our faith says so but just because it is right. Jesus, however, warned, "[W]hoever denies me before men, I also will deny before my Father who is in heaven" (Mt 10:33). In time, this can lead to a cascading spiritual tumble backward.

Or, by grace, we can accept this rejection as nothing more than what is to be expected and accepted as a follower of Jesus Christ, and move to step 9,[8] when, by grace, we accept whatever persecution comes because we stand with Jesus ("Blessed are you when men revile you and persecute you and utter all kinds of evil against you falsely on my account"). Our reward, for which we are to "rejoice and be glad", is eternal union with Christ in heaven. Until then, however, we can still fall back, when we realize that these steps have not led to a comfortable plateau; that we haven't reached an end at which we can rest in peace, knowing that we've arrived. Rather, we have merely reached the stage of discovering our lifelong mission, the "obedience of faith" in which we are called to live by grace every day until Christ calls us home.

We can become complacent in our presumptions, assuming that, through our efforts in obedience to Christ, we have arrived, and as a result we can blindly fall backward, glorying in our successes, even arrogantly wallowing in the external symbols of our spiritual progress.

Or, by grace, we can continue living the steps, which must be revisited and renewed every day, following Saint Paul's example, mentioned many times throughout this book:

> Not that I have already obtained this or am already perfect; but I press on to make it my own, because Christ Jesus has made me his own. Brethren, I do not consider that I have made it my own; but one thing I do, forgetting what lies behind and straining forward to what lies ahead, I press on toward the goal for the prize of the upward call of God in Christ Jesus. Let those of us who are mature be thus minded; and if in anything you are otherwise minded, God will reveal that also to you. Only let us hold true to what we have attained. (Phil 3:12–16)

Admittedly, these steps as presented are intimidating; each alone can seem out of reach, let alone a step to the next. Just making any headway toward detaching ourselves from the world seems impossible in this age when our very existence seems dependent on technologies, politics, and economic entanglements that those first-century

---

[8] We often hear of the eight Beatitudes, but there are those who speak of nine. I chose nine here because it seems as if Jesus was prophetically pointing to what has too often happened historically: believers step out into the world to do good deeds for righteousness' sake but then are hesitant to do so in the name of Christ. Acknowledging these as two intentions allows for a recognition of the necessary progress in courage and conviction.

Christians could never have imagined. The impossibility of these steps, in fact, is why so many of Jesus' hearers refused to follow Him. Yet, Jesus did not back down from the importance of these challenges, for in the Sermon on the Mount, He said, "You, there-fore, must be perfect, as your heavenly Father is perfect" (Mt 5:48). He also said, though, that this radical living was to be augmented with prayer, fasting, and almsgiving (Mt 6:1–18) and that if we asked, sought, and knocked, He would help us (Mt 7:7–12).

Just realizing the significance and promise of these Beatitudes is a start; it is the self-affirming evidence that God's grace is at work. Any effort we make to at least begin detaching ourselves from the world, sin, and self initiates a hunger and thirst in our hearts for righteous-ness. This in turn can strengthen us to show at least some mercy, which gives us a glimmer of the presence of God, which by grace can give us the courage to begin stepping out in His Name. This whole process involves little steps, day by day, inch by inch, until, by grace, these steps become habitual—virtues. So said Thomas à Kempis: "Each day we should renew our resolution, and bestir our-selves to fervour, as though it were the first day of our conversion, and say, 'Help me, O Lord God, in my good resolve and in your holy service: grant me this day to begin perfectly, for hitherto I have accomplished nothing.'"[9]

Three Stages of Conversion and Reconciliation

Understanding the Beatitudes as nine steps or rungs of contin-ual conversion has many parallels to how the spiritual life has been described throughout the history of the Church. For example, the nine steps correspond quite nicely to the traditional three stages of conversion or growth in the spiritual life.[10] The first three Beatitudes entail detachment, emptying oneself of attachments to the world, sin, and self. The staircase to heaven requires passing through suffering and sacrifice. (Even in gardening, before one can plant, one must

[9] Thomas à Kempis, *The Imitation of Christ*, 48.

[10] The purgative, the illuminative, and the unitive; see, for instance, Reginald Garrigou-Lagrange, O.P., *The Three Ages of the Interior Life.*

expend much energy in removing the deleterious attachments present in the soil.) In the second three Beatitudes, we are filled with the new, more rightly directed attachments to Christ: righteousness, mercy, and intimacy with God. The last three Beatitudes involve living out our attachment to Christ in love of neighbor, stepping out into the world as peacemakers, Christlike messengers of the gospel, accepting by grace whatever ridicule or persecution the world has to give.

This interpretation of the Beatitudes has a practical application, for almost everything Christ taught was directed at restoring broken relationships, with God and with others. When we experience a broken relationship, with a spouse, a family member, or a friend, the Beatitudes can provide a step-by-step path to reconciliation:

Dying to self

1st   Recognize that everything we have is a gift of God (gratitude).

2nd   Recognize our guilt for our sins and the misuse of God's gifts (remorse).

3rd   Recognize our pride, which exacerbates difficulties in the relationship that is suffering (humility).

Adopting the mind of Christ

4th   Do what is right in the eyes of God (love).

5th   Turn the other cheek (relinquish the "right to justice" and show mercy).

6th   Pursue purity of soul and the grace to stand without blemish before God.

Acting as Christ would

7th   Take action to restore peace, in imitation of God.

8th   Stand firm in the face of whatever rejection may come for acting according to God's commands.

9th   Accept without retaliation ridicule for our faith in Christ.

This may seem idealistic, even insurmountable, but again, like conversion, it is a process empowered by grace through faith. Reconciliation begins with ourselves: by setting our hearts and minds in the direction of reconciliation, it then shapes our prayer until it sets our convictions and our wills, until we step out and make peace with family, friends, and neighbors.

Rewards?

What about those rewards Jesus promised? It's crucial to understand that these steps, as well as everything mentioned in this book, are not meant to be guaranteed methods for earning or working our way to heaven. Rather, this path is what it *means* to believe, to have faith.

When Saint Paul wrote in Ephesians to those newly baptized convert pagans that "by grace you have been saved through faith, and this [was] not your own doing" (2:8), he was not specifically referring to the salvation they might one day experience at the end of their earthly lives, if by grace and perseverance they remained faithful. Rather, he was saying that it was the grace and mercy of God that had reached them and awakened them to truth, while they were yet lost in their attachments to the world, sin, and themselves, outside the Church (cf. Rom 5:6–11). As Father Jean Nicolas Grou wrote many years ago, our focus must not be on whether, as a result of our efforts, even our faith, we will be "saved", for in essence this can grow to become a self-centered quest; we can wrongly become attached to a myopic, self-motivated quest to reach heaven. Rather, our focus is to be, first, on giving glory to God; second, on growing by grace in holiness (the steps of the Beatitudes); and then, third, our happiness, entrusting our eternal destiny in hope to the mercy of our heavenly Father.[11]

[11] See Jean Nicolas Grou, S.J., *Marks of True Devotion with the Christian Sanctified by the Lord's Prayer* (Springfield, Ill.: Templegate, 1962); 8–13.

And so, those rewards? We are blessed! Our focus on Him and following Him in faithful obedience by grace, step by step, reap the blessings of his grace: "from his fulness have we all received, grace upon grace" (Jn 1:16).

Nurturing the Garden of Our Soul

What does any of this have to do with planting a garden or with our need to live each day as if it's our last or as long as God allows us to live? Since I began writing this chapter, I've made more trips out to the garden. I've cultivated a few more rows, planted potatoes and carrots, and watered each morning. I've also gone back daily to pluck out a few lingering or sprouting weeds. As a result, the vegetables are starting to flourish.

Growing a vegetable garden takes far more than the initial planting followed by months of leisure until the "judgment", when the crop is harvested. The garden needs daily care, inch by inch, row by row. If I were tending this garden for someone else, who had hired me to provide for him in September a luscious truckload of produce, he might stop by on any given day, unannounced, to see whether I was being a good steward of his land.

The steps of the Beatitudes are the means by which we nurture the garden of our soul every day, weeding out deleterious attachments so that grace can grow into righteousness, mercy, purity, and love. Since we don't know which day the Vinedresser will return (see Jn 15), we must repeat and continue this weeding and nurturing process every day for the rest of our lives—not merely as individuals, but in community, aided by the graces of the Word and sacraments— inch by inch and row by row.

15

Salvation Is Nearer Than You Think

Besides this you know what hour it is, how it is full time now for you to wake from sleep. For salvation is nearer to us now than when we first believed.

—Romans 13:11

Not long after turning sixty-one, I was on a long drive across Ohio in my pickup truck. Generally, I prefer the off-the-beaten-path country roads to the overcrowded expressways and turnpikes. At least in northwestern Ohio, the straightest routes are typically the back roads.

I also love these country roads because as I drive along, I pass farm after farm, fields nearly as far as the eye can see, interspersed by woods and orchards, ponds and pastures, cattle, horses, and sheep, all representing how farmers have tried to use what God has given them for the welfare of their families. Not all of them see it exactly this way, but nonetheless everything they possess they have received through the providence of God. "What have you that you did not receive?" (1 Cor 4:7b).

On this particularly long trip, I whiled away the hours by listening to one of my favorite old radio programs on satellite radio, *Lights Out*. As usual, the program began with the announcer saying, very slowly, in a droll monotone, "It . . . is . . . later . . . than . . . you . . . think." An interviewer once asked the author of the series what he meant by this statement. Dispelling any hopes of a profound hidden meaning, the author admitted that he merely saw this once written across an old stone sundial.

This vaguely reminded me of a Scripture text. At a stop sign, with no traffic in any direction as far as the eye could see, I reached for my Bible and, using the concordance, found the text in Romans: "Besides this you know what hour it is, how it is full time now for you to wake from sleep. For salvation is nearer to us now than when we first believed" (Rom 13:11). Translated into the slogan of that old radio show, this becomes:

Salvation ... is ... nearer ... than ... you ... think!

If for each one of us salvation is nearer than we think—if, say, we were told we had only five years to live, or maybe only a year or a month or a week, or what if the Master came home tonight and we found ourselves standing before God—then what is it, when all of our lives are laid before us and before Him, that is most important? What is it that will make any eternal difference from this life into the next?

As I kept driving across Ohio in that pickup truck, enjoying the beauty of the endless rolling farmland on both sides of the road, corn easily up to my truck's roof, all expressions of the endless efforts of farmers, farmhands, and their families, I reflected on that verse from Romans, and an analogy came to mind, one that I call the parable of the game.

Imagine that a highly respected, wealthy neighbor invites you to spend an evening at his mansion playing a board game—say, Farm-Opoly—and you accept. All evening, the game proceeds as usually played, and you and your opponents experience the usual wax and wane of material success. Drinks and snacks are passed and shared. At times, the game becomes quite heated as players bicker and barter for progress, position, and power. In the end, you are quite successful, but when your host declares the evening over, all the board money and game pieces are put away in the box, and you and the other players leave and return to your separate lives.

To what extent do the successes and failures that you attained in playing the game affect the rest of your life?

If you made millions in board game money and acquired acres of board game property, thereby gaining great board game influence, power, and prestige, or, on the other hand, if you lost everything and spent most of the game in jail, what difference does any of this make to the real life you lead once you've put all the game pieces back into the box, closed it, and placed it on the shelf?

At first thought, nothing. Nothing you or anyone accomplishes or accumulates in the playing of a board game—successes or failures, gains or losses—carries over into real life outside the box.

Yet this is not exactly true.

It seems to me that there are at least *seven things* (there's that biblical number of perfection again!) that do carry over to real life:

1. *How we treated those we played with.* If we acted like jerks, cheated, lied, and generally, in our self-centeredness, stepped on everyone else in the game, we might find that none of them will want to speak to us again. They might never see us in the same way, and the host will certainly not invite us back.

2. *How our actions indirectly affected those we played with.* There is something in gaming called a zero-sum gain: if we are winning, someone else has to be losing; if we are gaining stuff, someone else is losing stuff. If in the playing, we were driven by the goal of accumulation and power, with no concern for how our actions were affecting the others around us, again, we might find that we have lost friends, gained a less-than-shining reputation, and nixed any future invitations to the mansion.

3. *How we ourselves changed from what we learned about ourselves in the playing.* In the process, did we discover any flaws in our character, and then did we try to change? When the game was over, were we any different or just the same?

4. *How we treated the game area.* Was there a ring of trash around our corner of the table? Potato chip crumbs, popcorn kernels, spilled beer, crumpled and torn board game money, chocolate on the tablecloth, mud on the carpet? If so, none of those friends, let alone the host, might ever invite us to their homes.

5. *How we enjoyed playing the game.* Were we always angry, complaining, bitter, discontent, or depressed, or did we seek the joy in the very privilege of

having been invited and having the opportunity to enjoy the time with friends, even if we spent the entire game in jail?

6. *How others remember how we played the game.* This is the issue of legacy. When the group gathers in the future, how do they remember how we played? Did we leave an example to follow, maybe a better way than has ever been played, or did we leave an example that everyone has sworn to avoid?

7. *How grateful we were to the host.* Did we storm out or leave ungraciously without a word to the host, or were we thankful for the privilege of the invitation?

This parable of the game is a parable of life. In the parable, playing the game represents life in this world, and the real life outside the game represents our life in the kingdom of God.

Once the game of this life is put away in the box, what remains and affects our life in the kingdom?

Our Lord proclaimed to His apostles that, if we are *in Him*, we are no longer "of the world, even as [He was] not of the world" (Jn 17:14). Anyone in Christ has become a citizen of the kingdom, "with the saints and members of the household of God" (Eph 2:19), and is called by Christ to become detached from the things of this world. Thomas à Kempis wrote:

> Here you have no abiding city, and wherever you may be, you are a stranger and pilgrim; you will never enjoy peace until you become inwardly united to Christ.
>
> What do you seek here, since this world is not your resting place? Your true home is in Heaven; therefore remember that all the things of this world are transitory. All things are passing, and yourself with them. See that you do not cling to them, lest you become entangled and perish with them.[1]

This was built upon the words of our Lord: "He who loves his life loses it, and he who hates his life in this world will keep it for eternal life" (Jn 12:25); "For what will it profit a man, if he gains the whole world and forfeits his life?" (Mt 16:26). These seem like harsh words, but they warn us not to become inordinately attached to this

---

[1] Thomas à Kempis, *The Imitation of Christ* (New York: Penguin Books, 1982), 68.

world. As C.S. Lewis warned in his classic *Mere Christianity*, "Aim at Heaven and you will get earth 'thrown in'; aim at earth and you will get neither."[2]

If this is the danger, then it might seem as if it would have been better if Jesus had immediately taken His followers home with Him. But that was not God's plan. These new citizens of the kingdom had an important job to do: to be messengers in this world (see Jn 17:11–18), or as Saint Paul described, "ambassadors" (2 Cor 5:17–21), to help others, those lost in this world and attached to it, to discover their need to become citizens of the kingdom, through faith in Jesus Christ and baptism into membership in His Mystical Body, the Church.

What does it mean *practically*, though, that we are children of God, citizens of the kingdom and not citizens of this world, of this "box", this "game"? Did Jesus leave us in this world to become successful and powerful? To accumulate riches and property so that we can spend what time we've been given here in comfort, luxury, and easy living? To eat, drink, and be merry, because when life is done, we leave it all behind us anyway?

No, for as our Lord said in His Sermon on the Mount:

> For all the nations of the world seek these things; and your Father knows that you need them. Instead, seek his kingdom, and these things shall be yours as well.
> Fear not, little flock, for it is your Father's good pleasure to give you the kingdom. Sell your possessions, and give alms; provide yourselves with purses that do not grow old, with a treasure in the heavens that does not fail, where no thief approaches and no moth destroys. For where your treasure is, there will your heart be also. (Lk 12:30–34)

When our time in this world is over, when all we have accomplished and accumulated in this life is put away in the "box", then what? Saint Paul warned that "we must all appear before the judgment seat of Christ, so that each one may receive good or evil, according to what he has done in the body" (2 Cor 5:10). The same warning was given in the book of Revelation:

> And I saw the dead, great and small, standing before the throne, and books were opened. Also another book was opened, which is the

[2] C.S. Lewis, *Mere Christianity* (New York: Harper Collins, 2001), 159.

book of life. *And the dead were judged by what was written in the books, by what they had done....* And if any one's name was not found written in the book of life, he was thrown into the lake of fire. (20:12, 15, emphasis mine)

As mentioned in an earlier chapter, our Lord explained this even more clearly in a parable:

"Take heed, and beware of all covetousness; for a man's life does not consist in the abundance of his possessions." And he told them a parable, saying, "The land of a rich man brought forth plentifully; and he thought to himself, 'What shall I do, for I have nowhere to store my crops?' And he said, 'I will do this: I will pull down my barns, and build larger ones; and there I will store all my grain and my goods. And I will say to my soul, Soul, you have ample goods laid up for many years; take your ease, eat, drink, be merry.' But God said to him, 'Fool! This night your soul is required of you; and the things you have prepared, whose will they be?' So is he who lays up treasure for himself, and is not rich toward God." (Lk 12:15–21)

When all is done, and we stand before God, when the Book of Life is opened, when the fruit of our lives is examined, what will be important? I believe, given that "salvation ... is ... nearer ... than ... you ... think", that it is crucial that we consider the importance of those same seven points from the parable of the game, but in a slightly different order:

1. *How we loved God.* This is summarized in what is called the Great Commandment: "[Y]ou shall love the Lord your God with all your heart, and with all your soul, and with all your mind, and with all your strength" (Mk 12:30). How grateful were we to the Host, to the Father through Jesus Christ by the power of the Holy Spirit, for all that He has given us, which means everything, every opportunity to know, love, and serve Him?

As an Evangelical minister, I would have expressed it this way: "Do you have a personal relationship with Jesus Christ?" Maybe surprisingly, this is precisely how Pope Emeritus Benedict XVI put it: "And this, dear brothers and sisters, is true for every Christian: faith is first and foremost a personal, intimate encounter with Jesus; it is having an experience of his closeness, his friendship, his love. It is in this way that we learn to know him ever better, to love and follow him more and more. May this happen to each one of us!"[3]

As Pope Francis also said, "True wealth is love of God, shared with others.... Who experiences this does not fear death, and receives peace of heart."[4]

This is a consistent theme throughout Scripture. For example, after Saint James reminded us that as "the sun rises with its scorching heat and withers the grass; its flower falls, and its beauty perishes ... [s]o will the rich man fade away in the midst of his pursuits", he then affirmed, "Blessed is the man who endures trial, for when he has stood the test he will receive the crown of life which God has promised to those who love him" (1:11–12).

A chapter later, Saint James made it even clearer, saying in one simple sentence what I have struggled to say throughout this entire book: "Has not God chosen those who are poor in the world to be rich in faith and heirs of the kingdom which he has promised to those who love him?" (2:5).

It's essential to recognize that this Christian understanding of love or charity is not referring to an emotion or feeling but rather an act of the will. We cannot choose to feel the emotions of love; but in choosing to act in love, the feelings of affection can grow. C. S. Lewis wrote, "Ask yourself, 'If I were sure that I loved God, what would I do?' When you have found that answer, go and do it."[5]

2. *How we loved our neighbor.* This is what is called the second Great Commandment: "You shall love your neighbor as yourself", and our Lord added, "There is no other commandment greater than these" (Mk 12:31). When all the great industrialists, bankers, inventors, and investors die, what will ultimately matter will not be

---

[3] Pope Benedict XVI, general audience, October 21, 2009, http://www.vatican.va/holy
_father/benedict_xvi/audiences/2009/documents/hf_ben-xvi_aud_20091021_en.html.

[4] Pope Francis, Angelus message, August 4, 2013, as quoted in "Pope Calls on Young People to Counter Daily Vanity of Consumer Society", *AsiaNews.It,* http://www.asianews.it /news-en/Pope-calls-on-young-people-to-counter-daily-vanity-of-consumer-society -28655.html.

[5] C. S. Lewis, *Mere Christianity,* 132.

all the great things they made, accumulated, and accomplished, for all that will stay in the box. Rather, what will matter is how they loved their wives, children, families, friends, and neighbors, as well as the people they worked with. Thomas à Kempis wrote, "Without love, the outward work is of no value; but whatever is done out of love, be it ever so little, is wholly fruitful. For God regards the greatness of the love that prompts a man, rather than the greatness of his achievement."[6]

This, too, will be the measure of our lives. As Saint Francis of Assisi once said, "Men lose all the material things they leave behind them in this world, but they carry with them the reward of their charity and the alms they give. For these they will receive from the Lord the reward and recompense they deserve."[7]

As in the previous point, this love for neighbors is not primarily a feeling of affection but an act of the will. We are called to love even those we do not like, even our enemies. In this sense, we can apply the previous quote from C.S. Lewis like this: "Ask yourself, 'If I were sure that I loved [my spouse, my children, my coworker, the neighbor I hardly like], what would I do?' When you have found that answer, go and do it."[8]

This is what I tried to say in a previous chapter: we take the narrow path by becoming *in Christ*, and we continue along *abiding*, but in the end, entry through the narrow gate comes through *love*.

3. *How we indirectly loved others.* How did the way we spent our money, invested our time, and applied our talents affect other people in this world, people we didn't even know? If our ambition for power, position, prosperity, and wealth caused us to step on even one person, I believe that, in the end, when the books are opened and everything we have done in this life is examined, that person will be there at the judgment, pointing out, as Nathan did to David, "You are the man" (2 Sam 12:7).

How many people around the world, whom we will never know personally, have been affected by how we have spent our money,

---

[6] Thomas à Kempis, *The Imitation of Christ*, 43.

[7] Saint Francis to all the faithful, in *Opuscula Sancti Patris Francisci Assisiensis* (Florence: Quaracchi, 1949), 87–94; quoted in *Liturgy of the Hours*, vol. 4, Office of Readings for October 4, Feast of Saint Francis of Assisi.

[8] C.S. Lewis, *Mere Christianity*, 132.

by what we have said, or by what we have done in this life? Or maybe what we haven't but should have done?

4. *How we grew in grace.* What have we learned about ourselves, if we were listening, and how have we responded? How have we changed? Or have our lives been one continual disclaimer that we are without faults (cf. 1 Jn 1:8) or that it was always someone else's fault? As Saint Paul warned, "Put to death ... what is earthly in you" (Col 3:5).

5. *How we cared for what we were given (stewardship).* When Saint James warned that "friendship with the world is enmity with God" (4:4), he did not mean a Gnostic rejection of this world, but a rejection of sinful attachments. This world was created good, and our temporary life in  this world is a good that we have received as a gift from above (see 1:17). Everything we have been given is good, including technology. Mankind has created nothing; we have only discovered how to use the gifts, treasures, knowledge, techniques, and abilities placed in creation for our use. The question will be: How did we use, take care of, share, invest in, and improve what we were given? When we take care of creation, we live out the divine life we have been given and share with God in His creative activity in this world.

Pope Francis said in one of his general audiences, "Cultivating and caring for creation is an instruction of God which he gave not only at the beginning of history, but has also given to each one of us; it is part of his plan; it means making the world increase with responsibility, transforming it so that it may be a garden, an inhabitable place for us all."[9]

In a more recent homily, he expanded on this: "I urge all to look at the world through the eyes of the Creator: the Earth is an environment to protect and a garden to cultivate. May the relationship between man and nature not be driven by greed, to manipulate and exploit, but may the divine harmony between beings and creation be

[9] Pope Francis, general audience, June 5, 2013, http://www.vatican.va/holy_father/francesco/audiences/2013/documents/papa-francesco_20130605_udienza-generale_en.html.

conserved in the logic of respect and care, so as to be placed at the service of brothers and sisters, of future generations as well."[10]

In the parable of the talents, the departing king gave his servants talents (or maybe more accurately "resources") according to their abilities. At the end of the parable is a strange statement: "For to every one who has will more be given, and he will have abundance; but from him who has not, even what he has will be taken away" (Mt 25:29). Does this seem fair? To the wealthy and gifted, more is given, but to the poor and less gifted, even what they have will be taken away?

There are various explanations, but I prefer this: God has given to us everything we have, but everything also brings with it increasing responsibilities, often far more than we ever expect! If we want a lot of stuff, we are free to go for it, but are we able and ready to accept and manage all the responsibilities that come with ownership? Buy a house, buy a hobby! Buy a farm, and you'll never have a moment when your work is done! Want to be the president of the United States or the richest man in world? Go for it! With either of these, we can accomplish much good, but can we handle it? Can we handle the temptations, the attachments, the responsibilities, and the pressures? Saint Francis, once a rich young man, recognized that he could not handle the responsibilities of anything, so he gave everything away! The truth is that even the little we have will, in the end, be taken away and left in the box.

6. *How content we were.* Jesus told His followers, "*[A]bide in my love ...* [so] that my joy may be in you, and that your joy may be full" (Jn 15:9, 11). When our lives are over and we look back, will we see that they were full of the joy of Christ, or of anxiety, bitterness, and

regret? Did we seek to imitate Saint Paul, who, though in chains, claimed, "Not that I complain of want; for I have learned, in whatever state I am, to be content" (Phil 4:11)?

[10] Pope Francis, "General Audience", April 22, 2015, https://w2.vatican.va/content/francesco /en/audiences/2015/documents/papa-francesco_20150422_udienza-generale.html.

7. *How our lives inspired others.* Imagine having your name for all time in the New Testament as one who was so "in love with this present world" that you deserted Saint Paul (see 2 Tim 4:10). When our children, grandchildren, and those who knew our deeds and words remember us, will how we lived be a legacy worth imitating?

As my truck left the sparse farmlands and entered the busy suburbs of my destination, several countering questions came to mind:

Some might complain, "But isn't this just works righteousness? And besides, what does it truly mean to love?" When good players gather to play a board game, they don't make up the rules as they go along. Instead, to avoid confusion and disagreement, they first look at the instructions inside the lid of the box. That is why Christ gave us His Church as "the pillar and bulwark of the truth" (1 Tim 3:15) and sent the Holy Spirit to guide her (see Jn 16:13).

As to the relationship between works and righteousness, faith and love, the "instructions inside the lid of the box" state that "faith apart from works is dead" (Jas 2:26), or as a joint Lutheran–Catholic statement put it, "We confess together that good works—a Christian life lived in faith, hope, and love—follow justification and are its fruits. When the justified live in Christ and act in the grace they receive, they bring forth, in biblical terms, good fruit.... Thus both Jesus and the apostolic Scriptures admonish Christians to bring forth the works of love."[11] Or, as I discussed earlier, *believing in Christ* involves more than faith *alone*; it also involves *being, abiding,* and *loving in Christ.*

This is quite important. Certainly, throughout the history of Christendom, millions of sincere believers, regardless of their particular theologies, have been moved by the words of Scripture and the model of Christ to live out their faith in love. But the danger of many of these theologies has been to draw believers into imbalanced and incomplete priorities: for example, an overemphasis on faith *alone* can detract from the necessity of holiness, sacrifice, suffering, and selfless love.

On the other hand, the *Catechism of the Catholic Church* warns that Catholics safely home in the Church can still miss the mark: "Even though incorporated into the Church, one who does not however

---

[11] Lutheran World Federation and the Catholic Church's Pontifical Council for Promoting Christian Unity, *Joint Declaration on the Doctrine of Justification* (1999), no. 37.

persevere in charity is not saved."[12] This is essentially and succinctly put by Thomas Howard in his book *On Being Catholic*:

> There is only one agenda for all of us Christians, namely, our growing into conformity to Jesus Christ, that is to say, our being made perfect in Charity. We must all appear before the judgment seat of Christ, and at that tribunal there is not one test for Protestants and another for Catholics. All of us have arrived there by grace, and all of us are "washed in the blood of the Lamb", and all of us are to have been configured to Christ.[13]

To a very significant extent, all sin is a failure to love; all divisions and schisms are a failure of charity; and all abuse and misuse of God's creation is a failure to love Him.

From the earliest days of the Church, men and women have tried to augment, qualify, simplify, and, if nothing else works, replace the central message of the gospel. In response to Galatian believers who had been lured away by just such a "different gospel", Saint Paul wrote, "O foolish Galatians! Who has bewitched you, before whose eyes Jesus Christ was publicly portrayed as crucified?" (3:1). Since it is highly unlikely that any of the Galatians had been present in Jerusalem at the Crucifixion, then to what was Saint Paul referring? It might be that he meant the mental images of Christ's Crucifixion as created through the preaching of apostolic eyewitnesses, or maybe the liturgical presentation of Christ crucified, especially through His Real Presence in the Eucharist. Given the evidence we have of early Christian inscriptions and art, is it possible, however, that Saint Paul was referring to that which has been displayed in the front of Church sanctuaries throughout Christendom ever since: the purest example of charity "publicly portrayed"—a crucifix?

When Christians denigrate the crucifix because they think it denies the Resurrection of Christ, they sadly are missing the point, for a crucifix would be meaningless except for the fact of the Resurrection. In a similar vein, when modern Catholics replace the suffering Christ with a resurrected Christ, I believe they, too, can be missing the point. Certainly Saint Paul believed in the Resurrection

---

[12] *Catechism of the Catholic Church* (*CCC*), 2nd ed. (Vatican City: Libreria Editrice Vaticana, 1997), no. 837.

[13] Thomas Howard, *On Being Catholic* (San Francisco: Ignatius Press, 1997), 147.

even though he said, "I decided to know nothing among you except Jesus Christ and him crucified" (1 Cor 2:2). The reason, however, for the constant insistence of the public portrayal of the crucifix is not just to remind us of the self-emulation of Christ on the Cross but to confront us with the true meaning of love. Faith in Christ means looking upon the "publicly portrayed" image of His sacrifice and being willing to do the same for Him. This is precisely how Jesus defined what it means to be His follower: "This is my com-

mandment, that you love one another as I have loved you. Greater love has no man than this, that a man lay down his life for his friends" (Jn 15:12–13). Elsewhere in Galatians, Saint Paul confessed what this radical love meant for him:

> I have been crucified with Christ; it is no longer I who live, but Christ who lives in me; and the life I now live in the flesh I live by faith in the Son of God, who loved me and gave himself for me.... But far be it from me to glory except in the cross of our Lord Jesus Christ, by which the world has been crucified to me, and I to the world. (2:20; 6:14)

Faith in Christ means loving in the same way He loved us. That really hits home, for this is how Saint Paul defined how I, as a husband and father, am to love: "Husbands, love your wives, as Christ loved the church and gave himself up for her" (Eph 5:25).

As I pulled into my destination, I reconsidered that opening verse from Romans: "Besides this you know what hour it is, how it is full time now for you to wake from sleep. For salvation is nearer to us now than when we first believed" (13:11).

I then thought again of that verse in Hebrews about being "surrounded by so great a cloud of witnesses" (12:1) and was reminded that it was high time to quit procrastinating and start acting! These *witnesses* are not just the heavenly hosts, angels, martyrs, and saints, who are watching and cheering us on, but our spouses, children, grandchildren, friends, neighbors, coworkers, even the viewers, hearers, and readers of our high-sounding words—all of these are waiting to see whether we live out faithfully all of the things we teach, or as Saint John said in those letters to those churches, whether we "conquer".

May God grant us the grace and mercy to (1) know, love, and serve Him; (2) love one another; (3) consider how our actions and lifestyles affect people we will never know; (4) grow in holiness; (5) respect responsibly the things we have been given; (6) be content with a minimum of things, yet detached from them; and (7) leave behind a model for our children and grandchildren to follow, in Christ, amen.

16

How Can We Know What's True?

*Jesus then said to the Jews who had believed in him, "If
you continue in my word, you are truly my disciples, and
you will know the truth, and the truth will make you free."*

—John 8:31–32

Throughout this short book, I've shared examples from nature and life on our land to illustrate spiritual lessons. But how can you or I know whether any of these interpretive lessons are true and trustworthy? The bookstores and the Internet are overflowing with books and blogs by authors who use examples from nature to prove all kinds of things, from Christian truth to Hinduism, Buddhism, the New Age, even atheism; from investment strategies to leadership principles to political plat-  forms to dietary assumptions to parenting ideals to new moral codes. Nature has been used to justify some of the most radically contradictory ideals, from extreme isolationist pacifism to radical social Darwinism; and even to deny the viability of the family, marriage, and monogamous relationships.

So, yes, there is truth to be found and lessons to be learned by studying nature, but how can we be certain that what we've gleaned is trustworthy and ought to be passed down to our children? How can you be certain that I'm not just using examples from life out in the country to justify some hidden personal agenda?

188

For example, consider once again this analogy from life on our land. After living here only a year, we had discovered gems, "hidden treasure", "pearls of great value", if you will, that others might curse as nothing more than pesky brambles. As I mentioned earlier, every year our greatest crop—our most precious natural resource—has been hundreds of wild black raspberry and blackberry bushes. Last year we picked dozens of quarts, and even then we could not keep up with the "crop" as it ripened.

Remember that section of land I said we had stripped bare but neglected to reseed? It grew back infested with wild, luscious raspberries and blackberries. But God certainly did not make these precious berries easy to pick! These acres of pearls are also acres of thorns. Likewise, the gifts that God has given each of us to enjoy, develop, and use for His glory require discipline and sacrifice and often involve suffering. As Scripture teaches, "We are children of God, and if children, then heirs, heirs of God and fellow heirs with Christ, *provided we suffer with him* in order that we may also be glorified with him" (Rom 8:16–17, emphasis mine).

The idea for seeing the infestation of our land with fruit-bearing brambles as acres of hidden treasure or pearls of great value is loosely based on two familiar parables of the kingdom: "The kingdom of heaven is like treasure hidden in a field, which a man found and covered up; then in his joy he goes and sells all that he has and buys that field. Again, the kingdom of heaven is like a merchant in search of fine pearls, who, on finding one pearl of great value, went and sold all that he had and bought it" (Mt 13:44–46).

Russell Herman Conwell, a Baptist minister who lived from 1843 to 1925, was the creator of "Acres of Diamonds", a phenomenally successful lecture loosely based on these verses. He personally delivered this lecture over six thousand times, acquiring over four million dollars in earnings. With this, he founded Temple University and Conwell School of Theology (which later was combined with Gordon Divinity School to become Gordon-Conwell Theological Seminary, my alma mater).

What is the correct interpretation and application, however, of Jesus' "hidden treasure" or "pearl of great price"? My admittedly personal and lighthearted application? Or what proved to be Russell Conwell's quite lucrative Baptist interpretation, or that of other

Protestants, or even that of other Baptists? Or what about the interpretations of Catholics, Orthodox, or other Christians, not to mention *The Pearl of Great Price*, a foundational Mormon book based on this text that has a radically different perspective from all the others combined?

How does one determine whose opinion on any of the things I've discussed is authoritatively and trustingly true?

At some point, when I was a young man, a switch in my brain turned on, and I began to desire to know, follow, and then proclaim "the truth". In the late sixties, I sought truth and proclaimed what I had found through folk music, and as any of us past sixty might remember, folk music hardly had a consistent and reliable theme!

In the early seventies, I turned to science and thought I had found trustworthy assurance in scientific materialism. Chemistry, physics, and especially ecology and environmentalism were the underlying truths that I believed could explain and give meaning to life. Save the planet! But in seeking to save the planet, I came to realize that we were ultimately denuding all meaning from life itself. If we are nothing but the accidental concoctions of water and chemicals, and meaningless electrical impulses and hormonal passions, then truth itself is but a vapor: nothing to be followed let alone proclaimed. As Steve Nicholls admits in his book *Paradise Found*, "Good and evil, fairness and unfairness have no meaning at all in a world shaped by natural selection."[1]

Then by God's grace and mercy, I rediscovered the faith of my childhood. My heart and mind were changed. I had found a truth worth living and dying for. From then on, I believed truth could be found only through reading the Scriptures, for our Lord said, "If you continue in my word, you are truly my disciples, and you will know the truth, and the truth will make you free" (Jn 8:31–32). Until I was forty years old, and ten years a Protestant minister, I never wavered from this conviction. How can one know what is true? Through the one trustworthy source: the Bible *alone*. Read the Bible every day, pray it, memorize it, know it, and with the help of the Holy Spirit, you will know what is true and necessary for salvation. But does this work?

---

[1] Steve Nicholls, *Paradise Found* (Chicago: University of Chicago Press, 2009), 427.

In seminary, I was taught a process to ensure that what I proclaimed on Sundays would be biblically true, and I had diligently followed this process since my ordination. On Monday mornings, I would begin preparation by making a fresh English translation, from Greek or Hebrew, of whatever text I had scheduled for Sunday. I'd then fill pages with exegetical study notes and reflections. Once I had arrived at a tentative conclusion of the meaning of the passage, and a rough outline of my thoughts, only then would I consult the row of biblical commentaries on my shelf to ensure that my conclusions were on track.

One day it struck me: I had handpicked every commentary on my shelf, from the scholars I liked, whose theologies I agreed with. In other words, I was merely checking my conclusions against people I already agreed with. In essence, I was only checking myself against myself! I had protected myself from any way of knowing whether I was—or they were—wrong.

Then one Sunday morning as I was preaching, it dawned on me that within a thirty-mile radius of my pulpit, there were probably thirty other pastors in thirty other churches who also considered the Bible as the sole authority for our faith. The problem was that I knew we were all teaching different if not contradictory things, possibly on the same text. Which one of us was preaching *truth*?

As an evangelically minded Presbyterian Calvinist, I believed and preached "once saved, always saved": that once a person accepts Jesus Christ as Lord and Savior, he has arrived; he is saved by grace through faith *alone*, and because he has done nothing to earn salvation, there is likewise nothing he can do to lose it. This, however, was certainly not what the Methodist, Episcopalian, Wesleyan, Nazarene, or Disciples, let alone Roman Catholic, ministers around me believed or taught.

As I gazed week after week from my pulpit, I knew many of the intimate details of the lives of my congregation, especially my staff. I began to realize that my understanding of Scripture prevented me from challenging any of them to change their lives. Many of them needed to break from debilitating sin—as demanded in Scripture—and even more of them needed to live their faith more radically, but I had no theological grounds to challenge anyone—let alone any real authority to do so. Certainly, in obedience to Scripture, I called them to turn from sin and to Christ, but my harangues merely bounced off the glazed eyes of their presumptions. As mentioned earlier, the Protestant Reformers had essentially truncated the gospel merely to *being in Christ* by faith *alone*; *abiding in Christ* and *loving in Christ*, though important ways to demonstrate our faith in gratitude to Christ, were not deemed necessary for salvation.

This impotence was particularly evident in moral and life issues. Our Presbyterian denomination, like most mainline denominations, had gradually and democratically redefined the moral implications of the gospel, leaning more and more in a relativistic and pro-choice direction. Marilyn and I were both decidedly pro-life. She was the director of a crisis pregnancy center and, more often than not, found herself working beside Catholics whose views were far more in line with ours. I had also discovered that, through the dues that my congregation and I were paying to the head office of our denomination, we were funding abortions—for the daughters and wives of pro-choice ministers—and there was nothing we could do to stop this.

With this, I knew I could no longer be a Presbyterian. So I began reading an encyclopedia of Christian denominations—three hundred pages of all the different Christian traditions in America. One by one, I examined each tradition, and one after another, I rejected them. I found something in the theology or practice of each denomination that I could not accept as *true* to how I understood Scripture.

I received a phone call from a pastor friend who, in a panic, exclaimed, "Marcus, you can't leave the Presbyterian church! You must remain loyal, even if all the leaders have become heretics and the church is going down in flames: we need the faithful to remain loyal!" And I answered, "If that is true, then why did we leave our last denomination to form this one? And the division before that, and before that, and before that? Why does loyalty to *truth* require that I stand firm here in this denomination? Why not move on and form a *truer* church? Because in time, we both know that we would have to move on and form another one, and another one, and another ad infinitum."

You see, the motto of at least my Presbyterian heritage has always been "Reformed and always reforming". The way we reformed was through re-forming, starting one new church after another, until today even a Protestant source admits that there are over thirty thousand individual denominations in the world, growing at the rate of one new denomination every five days![2]

Then a dear friend pointed out a Scripture text from Saint Paul that I had never *seen* before:

> I hope to come to you soon, but I am writing these instructions to you so that, if I am delayed, you may know how one ought to behave in the household of God, which is *the Church of the living God, the pillar and bulwark of the truth.* (1 Tim 3:14–15, emphasis mine)

Scripture teaches that the Church is the "pillar and bulwark of the truth"? I had never given one thought to the necessity of the *Church* for knowing and discerning "the truth". But if Saint Paul was right, then *which* church? My Presbyterian denomination? But which Presbyterian denomination? My local congregation? Or the Lutheran, Methodist, Baptist, Episcopal, Pentecostal, et cetera, et cetera, denominations? Or which branch of these? But surely not the Catholic Church! And besides, as a Calvinist Protestant, I believed that the *true* Church was invisible, consisting of true believers all over the world, and that her membership was known only to God.

At that moment, it struck me: how could an invisible church, known only to God, be the pillar and bulwark of anything?

After much reflection, it became apparent that the key foundation of our Protestant faith, *sola Scriptura*, was not biblical, nor theologically or philosophically sound; in fact, the very Scriptures we used to defend the foundational doctrine did not teach it. Saint Paul had written that "all scripture is inspired by God and profitable for teaching, for reproof, for correction, and for training in righteousness" (2 Tim. 3:16). This does not, however, teach that Scripture is the sole authority of our faith; nor does Scripture itself define which books are to be included in this collection of inspired Scriptures.

Another friend of mine then pointed out *another* verse I had never seen, 2 Thessalonians 2:15: "Therefore, brethren, stand fast and hold the traditions which you were taught, whether by word or our epistle" (NKJV). *Tradition!* This verse spoke of the importance of passing

---

[2] David B. Barrett, George T. Kurian, and Todd M. Johnson, *World Christian Encyclopedia: A Comparative Survey of Churches and Religions in the Modern World*, vol. 1 (New York: Oxford University Press, 2001), 18.

on faithfully the apostolic tradition, which was received primarily through the spoken word and only occasionally through epistles when an apostle could not speak to his people directly.

We Evangelical Protestants denied the trustworthiness of any *tradition* as nothing more than the "traditions of men" (cf. Mk 7:8). Yet the reason there is no church in the world that actually lives out *sola Scriptura* is because every church interprets Scripture through the lens of its own passed-on tradition—the tradition of the founder of its movement. It was this nearly limitless assortment of traditions that has spawned the cacophony of opinions, including my own, coming from pulpits every Sunday.

As a result of my reflections, the Protestant foundation of *sola fide* also began to topple. I never questioned, from the time of my childhood Lutheran catechetical formation, that we are saved by faith *alone*, but another verse I had never taken seriously, James 2:24, got my attention: "You see then that a man is justified by works, and not by faith *only*" (NKJV, emphasis mine). This revelation concurred with what I had always known in my conscience to be true: we are not merely "once saved, always saved" through some one-time surrendering statement of faith in Christ; we must live this out by grace for the rest of our lives! Again, as Saint James wrote, "But be doers of the word, and not hearers only, deceiving yourselves" (1:22, NKJV).

I cannot give here a detailed account of how my wife and I came to believe that the Catholic Church is this "pillar and bulwark of the truth".[3] Allow me, however, to focus on the one issue that in the end closed the deal.

Jesus did not merely travel around preaching about the kingdom and encouraging every enthusiastic follower to teach likewise. Rather He selected twelve apostles and "gave them authority" (Mt 10:1). In every list of these twelve, the Gospel writers place Simon Peter first (see Mt 10:2), and there was a reason for this. To this first of the apostles, Jesus had said, "[Y]ou are Peter [Cephas, in Aramaic], and on this rock [Cephas] I will build my Church, and the gates of Hades shall not prevail against it. I will give you the keys of the kingdom of

---

[3] More details of our journey into the Catholic Church can be found in *Journeys Home*, 3rd ed. (Zanesville, Ohio: Coming Home Resources, 2011) and *Journey Home 2* (Zanesville, Ohio: Coming Home Resources, 2015).

heaven, and whatever you bind on earth shall be bound in heaven, and whatever you loose on earth shall be loosed in heaven" (Mt 16:18–19).

On the night when Jesus was betrayed by one of His own, He told His apostles, "These things I have spoken to you, while I am still with you. But the Counselor, the Holy Spirit, whom the Father will send in my name, he will teach you all things, and bring to your remembrance all that I have said to you" (Jn 14:25–26). In a general way, this promise cannot be true for every single Christian; otherwise why is there so much disagreement between Spirit-filled Christians over what is *true*? Rather, Jesus was promising His hand-chosen apostles, headed by Peter, that "when the Spirit of truth comes, he will guide you into all the truth" (Jn 16:13).

After the trial, Crucifixion, and burial of Jesus, Saint Paul wrote to the Christian believers in the city of Corinth:

> Now I would remind you, brethren, in what terms I preached to you the gospel, which you received, in which you stand, by which you are saved, if you hold it fast—unless you believed in vain. For I delivered to you as of first importance what I also received, that Christ died for our sins in accordance with the Scriptures, that he was buried, that he was raised on the third day in accordance with the Scriptures, and that *he appeared to Cephas [Peter], then to the twelve. Then he appeared to more than five hundred brethren at one time, most of whom are still alive, though some have fallen asleep. Then he appeared to James, then to all the apostles. Last of all, as to one untimely born, he appeared also to me.* (1 Cor 15:1–8, emphasis mine)

Here even Saint Paul affirms the primary position of Peter (Cephas), but this quotation also emphasizes why the Christian understanding of nature, of life and death, and of eternity is the most trustworthy: it is founded upon the eyewitness testimony to the risen Christ. The man Jesus, who was crucified for claiming to be the Son of God, has risen from the dead. All of His apostles, except John, died as martyrs for their witness to this fact. John died of old age, yet only after years of exile for his witness to the risen Christ. The key question: Would any person willingly accept brutal martyrdom for a lie?

After His death and Resurrection, before He ascended to the Father, Jesus commissioned His hand-chosen apostolic leaders, upon whom He had breathed the promised Holy Spirit (see Jn 20:21–23) to go forth and make disciples, "baptizing them in the name of the Father and of the Son and of the Holy Spirit, teaching them to observe all that I have commanded you" (Mt 28:19–20). In other words, Jesus taught His apostles, who, guided by the Holy Spirit, were to pass this on faithfully through preaching. New believers were to be enveloped into the fellowship of the Trinity (see 1 Jn 1:3), the Church, through baptism.

At Pentecost, when the Holy Spirit descended with power on Christ's apostles, Simon Peter took his responsibility to heart and preached the first Christian sermon. When his hearers exclaimed, "Brethren, what shall we do?" Peter responded, "Repent, and be baptized every one of you in the name of Jesus Christ for the forgiveness of your sins; and you shall receive the gift of the Holy Spirit" (Acts 2:37–38). Here we see all the elements of the beginning and continuity of the Church: our Lord to His apostles, led by Peter, empowered by the Holy Spirit to proclaim *the Word*, and new converts received into the Church through baptism, themselves empowered by the Spirit to proclaim.

Years later, Saint Paul instructed his apprentice bishop, Timothy, "what you have heard from me before many witnesses entrust to faithful men who will be able to teach others also" (2 Tim 2:2). Here we see the authority of Saint Paul, which he had received from Saint Peter (see Gal 1:18—2:10), to appoint and empower other men to protect and pass on the apostolic tradition.

Toward the end of the first century, Saint Clement, the fourth bishop of Rome, wrote a letter to the same Christians in Corinth. The forcefulness of this letter itself witnesses to a unique authority of the bishop of Rome over a gathering of believers six hundred miles away in a different country. In this letter, Saint Clement witnessed to this apostolic succession of passing on the truth:

> *The apostles received the Gospel for us from our Lord Jesus Christ, and Jesus Christ was sent from God.* So Christ was from God, and the apostles from Christ. So both came by the will of God in good order. Once they received commands, once they were made confident through the resurrection of our Lord Jesus Christ, and once they were entrusted with God's Word, they went out proclaiming with the confidence

of the Holy Spirit that the kingdom of God would come. Preaching in lands and cities, by spiritual discernment, they began establishing their first fruits, who were bishops and deacons for future believers. And this was nothing new because for many ages it had been written about bishops and deacons, as Scripture says somewhere, "I will appoint bishops for them in justice and deacons in faith."[4]

Then, toward the end of the second century, Saint Irenaeus, the bishop of Lyons, wrote a set of books entitled *Against Heresies* in which he gave witness to this continuity of apostolic authority:

> But since it would be too long to enumerate ... the successions of all the churches, we shall confound all those who ... assemble other than where it is proper, by pointing out here the successions of the bishops of the greatest and most ancient Church known to all, founded and organized at Rome by the two most glorious apostles, Peter and Paul, that Church which has the tradition and the faith which comes down to us after having been announced to men by the Apostles. *For with this Church, because of its superior origin, all Churches must agree, that is, all the faithful in the whole world*; and it is in her that the faithful everywhere have maintained the Apostolic tradition.[5]

This chapter is not meant to be a thorough apologetic for the truth of the Catholic Church—nor even a minimal attempt to answer all the objections one might raise against this claim, for the bitter opinions out there against Catholics and the Catholic Church are myriad. Rather, this is merely a way of addressing the big question of where I have come to believe a person can go to find a trustworthy source of authority and wisdom, whether he is trying to interpret the meaning of nature or the meaning of life. This book is but a sampling of why Marilyn and I have never questioned our decision to come home to the "acres of diamonds" established by Christ in His apostles, centered on the authority of Peter, in the Catholic Church.

As Pope Saint John Paul II said in the first sentence of his introduction to the *Catechism of the Catholic Church*, "Guarding the Deposit of Faith is the mission which the Lord entrusted to His Church, and

---

[4] Quoted in Kenneth J. Howell, *Clement of Rome and the Didache* (Zanesville, Ohio: Coming Home Resources, 2012), 115.

[5] Saint Irenaeus, *Against Heresies*, 3.2.2.

which she fulfills in every age."[6] This Deposit of Faith includes a clear social doctrine, on which I have tried to base the reflections in this short book. For those unfamiliar with the beauty and integrity of the Catholic Church's social teachings, I'm including the following broad overview.

The social doctrine of the Catholic Church rests upon ideas concerning (a) the character of God's plan of love for humanity, (b) the Church's salvific mission and its social responsibilities in light of that plan, and (c) the nature of the human person and corresponding human rights, supported by studies and interpretations of Scripture, over the course of two millennia, acknowledged to be authoritative by the Magisterium. The abiding principles comprising its backbone are the following.

1. God's salvific love for us grounds *the human dignity of all persons as children of God*. The principles of Catholic social doctrine flow from the well-spring of that God-founded dignity and urge us to "an integral and solitary humanism". They are ultimate organizing principles for life in society to be understood in their interrelatedness and unity. The diminishment of our own and others' human dignity, in a *de facto* and or *de jure* second-guessing of the value with which God has endowed us, is the ultimate personal and social sin.

2. Because of our dignity as children of God, we have a duty to discern and pursue *the common good* of the human community on a local, regional, national, and international level. We are called to do so in conscientious dialogue with the Church and its traditions. We cannot "go it alone", in our pride, defining the common good in whatever way may please us. Discernment for the common good is a properly communal activity requiring in-depth consideration and analysis from many different vantage points, not just our own.

3. *The goods of this earth have a universal destination*; they are meant for the genuine benefit and well-being of all of humanity, not just a privileged few. There is, accordingly, in certain circumstances of human need, a social mortgage even upon private property.

[6] Apostolic Constitution *Fidei Depositum* (On the Publication of the *Catechism of the Catholic Church*), October 11, 1992, in *Catechism of the Catholic Church*, 2nd ed. (Vatican City: Libreria Editrice Vaticana, 1997), 1.

4. *"Subsidiarity"* defines the optimal relationship among different levels of organization of human community and human activity. The more local control that human beings can exercise over their own affairs, in other words, the better. Such control allows people to develop confidence, competence, and a proper self-reliance and independence; it also creates the conditions best suited to the exercise of an authentic moral freedom by ensuring that people have as much constructive power over the factors shaping their lives as possible. Our political and economic structures, among others, should incorporate the principle of subsidiarity.

5. Everyone has a *duty to participate actively in the life of the human community* at its various levels and to make his or her contribution for the good, properly discerned. The exigency to participate includes full involvement as a responsible citizen in the political life of the community. It also includes, but is not limited to, a transformation of human work to serve the common good, properly discerned.

6. The *fundamental values of social life are truth, freedom, and justice.* Instrumental uses of other human beings to attain personal, selfish ends and the deceits and disregard for their humanity suiting such utilitarianism are completely alien to our Catholic values. Further, the freedom at stake is not ultimately the freedom to make any choice. It is the freedom to act, without impediment, in accordance with the highest capacities of one's nature to achieve the good. *The Freedom to be truly good is the only freedom that ultimately matters.* Human beings are called upon to overcome, in love and patience, both the internal, spiritual obstacles that derail them from the pursuit of the good, e.g., selfishness, grudges, anxieties, hang-ups, hatreds, ego ambition, etc., and the external obstacles that derail them from seeking and attaining the good, e.g., the difficulties that circumstances and other people may pose for the realization of such aspirations.

7. Being part of one human family, we have the obligation to stand in *solidarity* with one another—we must, in other words, alleviate the suffering of the vulnerable among us and actively work to help others become fully participating persons in the community. We are called to assist one another to achieve our highest individual and communal potentials for goodness. *Progress in goodness is the only true development* both for individuals and for communities on the local, regional, national, and international levels.

8. *The standard of love set by Christ on the cross is the highest and most universal standard of Catholic social ethics.* It is *a standard,* individually and communally, *of selflessness, and so freedom, in service to others, as we regard them in reference to God,* and leads us to excellence in all of our undertakings. Our human dignity and the social values of truth, freedom, and justice spring from this source. Without this kind of love, as 1 Corinthians 13 notes, we are nothing.[7]

One of the main things I've tried to admit in writing this book is that I don't think—in my blind acceptance and active embrace of our modern, industrial, progressivist culture—that I would have discovered the authentic call to gospel simplicity if I hadn't moved from the din of the city out to the demanding peace of our rural land.

In like matter, I don't think I would have *heard* the full truth of the gospel in my Evangelicalism, as good as it was. What I preached was true as far as it went, but it had been channeled down a potentially myopic dead end, through the Reformers' obsession with self-actualization. By reducing the gospel to faith alone, they truncated Christianity to being in Christ, essentially stopping spiritual growth at the beginning, and removed any necessity for abiding and loving in Christ (see chapter 13). Faith alone in Jesus blinded me to the more important and central issues of the gospel, and I never saw the need to dig deeper, due to the assumptions of "imputed righteousness" and "once saved, always saved". Through their devotion to Christ, sincere Bible-believing Christians hear the true call of the gospel, but dangerously, by not seeing the signal importance of abiding and the call to detached, humble love, they might not in the end attain intimacy with Christ.

Yet history demonstrates all too often how Catholics, from the pope on down to the lowliest layman, have also failed to live out the gospel, for Catholics can too often miss the point of their Catholicism. The point is not ritual or structure or triumphantly preserving the history, the saints, the sacraments, the devotions, and the authority. All of these, including faith in Christ alone, are to equip

[7] From Donna M. Adler, "A Brief Introduction to the Social Doctrine of the Catholic Church", *Wyoming Catholic Register,* December 2014, http://www.dioceseofcheyenne.org /CSD/docs/SocialTeachingColumnIntro.pdf.

us to fulfill the great commandments to love. The saving grace of the Eucharist, as Catholics say "amen" in their reception of the Body and Blood of Christ, as Christ demanded of His followers if they desire to "have eternal life" (see Jn 6:51–58), is not merely the faithful partaking of it as a Catholic, but the surrendering self-identification of one's union with the self-sacrifice of Christ for others: partaking is a vow of obedience to go and do likewise, to imitate Christ.

This is reiterated over and over in that devotional classic by Thomas à Kempis that has been declared by both Catholics and Protestants as likely the most popular book in history:

> Of what use is it to discourse learnedly on the Trinity, if you lack humility and therefore displease the Trinity? Lofty words do not make a man just or holy; but a good life makes him dear to God. I would far rather feel contrition than be able to define it. If you knew the whole Bible by heart, and all the teachings of the philosophers, how would this help you without the grace and love of God? "Vanity of vanities, and all is vanity," except to love God and serve Him alone. And this is supreme wisdom—to despise the world, and draw daily nearer to the kingdom of heaven.[8]

This is why I am glad to be a Catholic: not so I can somehow rest assured of salvation because I have come to know that Christ established the Church as "necessary for salvation" and consequently have "come home". Rather, it is because, by grace, I have come to realize that, in the arrogant, proud, self-assured, and independently concocted interpretation of biblical Christianity that I proclaimed from my Presbyterian pulpit, I likely would not have learned how to abide in Christ and especially how to love—and not received the necessary sacramental graces to do so, unless I had come home to the Church.

For this and many, many other reasons, Marilyn and I are glad to be home. And we ask Saint Isidore, the patron saint of farmers, to pray for us, that we might have even an inkling of the worthiness of a farmer.

---

[8] Thomas à Kempis, *The Imitation of Christ* (New York: Penguin Books, 1982), 27–28.

EPILOGUE

I implore you to love with me and, by believing, to run with me;
let us long for our heavenly country,
let us sigh for our heavenly home,
let us truly feel that here we are strangers.

—Saint Augustine

The aging city-slicker transplant—wannabe farmer trudges slowly up the hill from the barn to the house. Around him the trees are at peak color, as their chlorophyll has drained away, leaving behind the true brilliant reds, oranges, and yellows of the leaves. But he walks oblivious to all this, his head focused on the ground before him.

One might guess that he was contemplating the long list of chores that needed to be completed in preparation for the coming winter. Or that he was stressed out by disturbing local, national, and international news—failing economies, threatening disease epidemics, encroaching threats from radical Islamic terrorists, foreign governmental unrest on many fronts, our own national politics in disarray, even concerns over changes in the Church. Or possibly that he was worrying about his family or work, or about how he will support his family in retirement and the future. All of these are valid topics for his contemplation. But this doesn't explain his seeming serpentine path up the slope. One might posit that he had been dipping a bit too deeply into a stash of New Straitsville moonshine.

If you were to ask him, however, and he were to answer, you would discover that none of these concerns was occupying whatever brain cells remained in his aging mind. Rather, his family had recently acquired a new mongrel pup, whose toilet habits were still unpredictable. So, with the learned eye of aged wisdom, he was attempting to weave his way home precariously through the minefield.

I suppose another topic that might have rightly cornered his mind would be the contents of this book that he had the audacity to write and publish. It isn't merely that many of the ideas expressed are difficult to stomach by most Americans, even most Christians, but that he himself has struggled to live by them and carry them out. He knows from experience that it takes a whole lot longer to get out of debt than it does to get in; such is also true for growing in detachment, simplicity, holiness, and humility. Bad habits and lifelong entanglements are difficult to correct—even if you want to!

As the old man reached the porch, he sat down to catch his breath. Climbing that hill was a whole lot easier fifteen years ago, even when hauling two buckets of fresh milk. As he sat, he once again wondered whether he should let this book out of its stall and into the realm of public scorn.

Of course, I am that old man, and I can't deny that I've waffled over and over on the contents of this book. There's nothing in it that I disagree with or don't believe wholeheartedly—even if my family and I still have a long way to grow before we're living these ideals. But I also realize that most of the people I've known throughout my life would have problems with much of what I've said. So is this book worth publishing?

As I was completing the last month of editing, I was also reading two very fine books, both related to the themes in this book. The first was *Paradise Found: Nature in America at the Time of Discovery*, by Steve Nicholls. Nicholls is an award-winning producer for a number of series on PBS's *Nature*. His book is a fascinating examination of how the population and diversity of wildlife, fish, fowl, and fauna in North America have changed drastically over the past five hundred years, as reported in the diaries and writings of explorers, pioneers, naturalists, missionaries, et cetera. He particularly describes, with justifiable wonder, the symbiotic relationships that have existed in nature from time immemorial. I found this book almost impossible to put down.

The second was an audiobook that I listened to as I drove cross-country to attend the funeral of a dear friend. This was *Growing a Farmer: How I Learned to Live Off the Land*, by Kurt Timmermeister, a restaurateur who describes step by step how he moved from apartment living in downtown Seattle to life on a small working farm on Vashon Island, Washington. Like Steve Nicholls' book, Timmermeister's is quite detailed but is about growing to become a farmer, from starting a community supported agriculture gardening business, to beekeeping, to establishing fruit and nut orchards, to raising and butchering livestock, to starting a dairy, to sponsoring weekly gourmet suppers from his produce, and finally to developing his dairy into a local craft cheesery. There is much about Timmermeister's book to enjoy, but I must admit, as he described in glaring details so much of what I too have attempted over the past fifteen years, his words helped me remember why I'm not doing so much of what he was able to accomplish. Like the similar accounts given in the equally enjoyable books *The Dirty Life*, by Kristin Kimball, and *Up Tunket Road*, by Philip Ackerman-Leist, it might be that when they started, they were all at least twenty years younger than moi.

Certainly with books like these on the market, along with the others I mentioned in my preface, the question arises: Why yet another book about rural life out on the farm or out in nature? I guess it was what I found missing in these books that finally convinced me to write. I refuse to say anything negative about any of these authors or their books; in fact, I would consider it a great privilege to meet these authors and discuss the things we have shared in common. However, I believe that, with all their enthusiasm and determined reflections on their work and experiences, they seem to have missed the point and the underlying message of what was right there in front of their eyes—of what they had been given the privilege to experience. I don't know the personal faith lives of any of them, and I certainly don't presume to guess or to stand in judgment. Yet, throughout all these books, I came away feeling that the authors resisted making any connections between what they have discovered and experienced and the source and meaning of these discoveries and experiences. Timmermeister freely admits that he is nonreligious, and throughout his book, Nicholls rarely misses a chance to blame Christianity, Christians, and particularly Catholics, for using theology as an excuse to destroy nature; he also constantly expresses amazement over the miracles of natural selection and evolution, even at times speaking of evolution as if it were an all-powerful entity or giving the animals themselves credit for choosing to evolve in order to survive in changing environments.

These authors might rightly claim that making altruistic or spiritual reflections from their experiences was not the purpose of their writings. I guess I'm just a Johnny One Note; I could never write a practical manual on sustainable farming or knowing nature. For me, the words of Jesus say it all: "For what will it profit a man if he gains the whole world [by leaving the city to become a self-sustaining small farmer, eating only his own self-grown organic non-GMO produce and fighting against industrial progress to save the East Tennessee green-lipped snail darter from extinction], and loses his own soul?" (Mk 8:36, NKJV).

I would never claim my book is worthy to share a shelf with any of those fine books I mentioned. It is my hope, however, that my reflections might help at least one person recognize the fingerprints of God in the world around us and, as a result, turn toward Him in humble gratitude. I also believe that what we can discover in nature and in rural living can help us understand ourselves better and how we can live more freely in this changing world. It is also my hope that, through these discoveries, at least one heart might be opened by grace to the saving love of Jesus Christ and the fullness of His Church.

I now need to trudge back to the barn, carefully making my way down the hill through that minefield. Murphy's Law has set in again, for after completing several unanticipated barn chores, I returned to the house without the pipe wrench I had originally gone to fetch! Life is like that. We can get distracted by seemingly urgent things and miss the things that are truly the most important and essential. God loves you and created you to have a relationship with Him, through His Son, by the power of the Holy Spirit, as an adopted child in His family, the Church. Don't miss this great gift.